DOOM

LANDMARK VIDEO GAMES

The Landmark Video Games book series is the first in the English language in which each book addresses a specific video game or video game series in depth, examining it in the light of a variety of approaches, including game design, genre, form, content, meanings, and its context within video game history. The specific games or game series chosen are historically significant and influential games recognized not only for their quality of gameplay but also for setting new standards, introducing new ideas, incorporating new technology, or otherwise changing the course of a genre or area of video game history. The Landmark Video Games book series hopes to provide an intimate and detailed look at the history of video games through a study of exemplars that have paved the way and set the course that others would follow or emulate, and that became an important part of popular culture.

Myst and *Riven:* The World of the D'ni
by Mark J. P. Wolf

Silent Hill: The Terror Engine
by Bernard Perron

DOOM: SCARYDARKFAST
by Dan Pinchbeck

DIGITALCULTUREBOOKS, an imprint of the University of Michigan Press, is dedicated to publishing work in new media studies and the emerging field of digital humanities.

DAN PINCHBECK

THE UNIVERSITY OF MICHIGAN PRESS ▪ ANN ARBOR

Published in the United States of America by
The University of Michigan Press
Manufactured in the United States of America
♾ Printed on acid-free paper

2016   2015   2014   2013   4   3   2   1

A CIP catalog record for this book is available from the British Library.

Library of Congress Cataloging-in-Publication Data

http://dx.doi.org/10.3998/lvg.11878639.0001.001

Pinchbeck, Daniel.
    Doom : scarydarkfast / Dan Pinchbeck.
        p.   cm. — (Landmark video games)
    Includes bibliographical references and index.
        ISBN 978-0-472-07191-3 (cloth : alk. paper) — ISBN 978-0-472-05191-5 (pbk. :
alk. paper) — ISBN 978-0-472-02893-1 (e-book)
    1. Doom 64 (Game)   I. Title.
    GV1469.35.D68P56   2013
    794.8—dc23

                                                                            2012042610

Acknowledgments

It's a little daunting to write a book about *DOOM*. There's a mass of information out there, lovingly collated and compiled by an army of fans who have a vast knowledge about the game, and the challenge is doing justice to them as much as to the game itself. This book would simply not have been possible without them. The honor roll includes Ian Albert, George Bell, Tony Fabris, Ledmeister, Lee Killough, Nathan Lineback, Hank Leukart, Zeta000, and the many unaccredited authors of the *DOOM* Wiki. Special thanks also go to Jacek Dobrzyniecki, Rowan Kaiser, and Lara Sanchez Coteron for passing on old reviews (and translating them too).

Likewise, I have to pay tribute to the makers of the "greatest game ever made," who have been exceptionally generous and forthcoming. Tom Hall, Sandy Peterson, Bobby Prince, and John Romero were all only too happy to subject themselves to questions via phone and e-mail. Tom Hall also supplied the title of the book—big thanks for that! I'm writing this sitting on a balcony in Mesquite, Texas, looking out toward id Software's offices, where the team has been absurdly welcoming. John Carmack, Kevin Cloud, Matt Hooper, Todd Hollenshead, and Tim Willits were all happy to give up their time, and special thanks go to Donna Jackson, who made my visit such a pleasure. My overriding memory will be Tim's fantastically succinct summation of the difference between *Classic DOOM* and *DOOM 3* as moving from "I'm fucked!" to "I'm fucked in the dark!"

I also have to thank Mark J. P. Wolf and Bernard Perron, the series editors, for the opportunity to write this book and for invaluable comments during the editing process. Equally, colleagues at the University of Portsmouth should be thanked, particularly Steve Hand and David Anderson, both of whom were very patient with me as I vanished into *DOOM* world toward the end of the writing period. Thanks also go to friends and colleagues around the world who found themselves on the end of rants, arguments, and jet-lagged mumblings about the project. You know who you are.

Finally, thanks to the two most important people in my life: Jessica and Oscar. I love you, and I'd fight through the forces of Hell for either of you any day of the week.

Contents

Introduction

*There Are a Lot of People Totally Opposed to
Violence. They're All Dead.*

It was early 1994, and the core, as I remember it, was me and my friends Tom and Andy. Tom was the one with the PC. We used to get together in his room in the halls of residence, with the lights off, and play this new game he'd just got. Usually, he was a freak for role-playing games—most recently, a top-down steampunk set on Mars—and a group of us would occasionally pull an all-nighter on *Civilization* (MicroProse 1991), but that winter, there was really only one game: id's seminal shooter *DOOM*. It's difficult to overstate the impact *DOOM* had on us all. We'd all thoroughly enjoyed *Wolfenstein 3D* (id Software 1992), of course, but for a bunch of nineteen-year-olds in the pre-PlayStation era, *DOOM* just blew everything else into bloody gibs.

This is a book about the most important first-person game ever made, about the blueprint that has defined one of the most successful genres of digital gaming. It is about a controversial, hyperviolent, scary, funny, exciting game that manages to be both profoundly, self-congratulatory dumb and exceptionally clever at the same time. All this and a chaingun—what more could you ask for?

I love first-person games: I think they are the most engaging, furious, immersive digital game form, even when they deviate from the basic run-and-gun model carved out by *DOOM* and typified by recent shooters like *Bulletstorm* (People Can Fly 2011) and *Killzone 3* (Guerilla Games 2011). There is something absolutely unique about the direct mapping of your perception onto an avatar's, something really wonderful about how, in many ways, these games extend the rewarding simplicity of early arcade gaming into the most high-end edges of technological implementation. The contemporary first-person shooter *Crysis 2* (Crytek 2011) may look like an oil painting (if not actually better), but at heart, it's just first-person *Defender* (Williams Electronics 1981). Lurking just below the dystopian musings on free will and capitalism that give *Bioshock* (2K Boston + 2K Australia 2007) its unique flavor is *Wolfenstein 3D* with water and a wrench.

DOOM's legacy includes some of the finest moments in gaming yet produced. Without it, *Half-Life* (Valve Software 1998) wouldn't have pushed how story is delivered in games seismically forward or set the crowbar at a new high for level design. There would be no *Portal* (Valve Software 2007), no *Call of Duty: Modern Warfare 2* (Infinity Ward 2009), no *F.E.A.R.: First Encounter Assault Recon* (Monolith 2005), no *Mirror's Edge* (DICE 2008). The technological advances of *DOOM* cast an equally long, dynamically rendered shadow. Then there's the creation of the online multiplayer gaming scene, via id embracing the idea of players playing against one another over LANs and online networks. You could argue that maybe the entirety of the massively multiplayer economy owes something to *DOOM*. Finally, id's championing of the open-source ethos—not just through the adoption of the Apogee model but through opening up of build tools to fan communities—effectively created the modding scene, which has had a huge impact on gaming as a movement.

Enough hyperbole. I've made some pretty big claims here, and though I suspect that you don't really need convincing if you know anything about games, duty calls me to offer some evidence to back them up. So this is what we're going to do: examine the context that *DOOM* crawled into, bloody and triumphant; talk a little about id, the dark heart of the enterprise; and try to paint a picture of the game's impact on release. We're going to take a tour under the hood to look at what made *DOOM* so important as a piece of software engineering. Then it will be time to get down and dirty on Phobos, Deimos, and Hell itself and discuss level and experience design. In case all that isn't enough, there's some other work to do. We have to look into multiplayer in a little more detail, and we need to discuss mods. We need to talk about the ports, sequels, and reboots: *DOOM II* and particularly *DOOM 3*. So that's enough introduction: strap on your ammo bandolier, power up the plasma gun, grab some blue armor, and, in the immortal words of *DOOM*'s hilariously succinct intro, put a "couple of pellets in the forehead" of whatever killed your buddies.

Assuming, for just a minute, that you may have been living in a bunker for the last nineteen years, I need to make a formal introduction. *DOOM* is a first-person shooter. Its minimal heads-up display contains an ammo counter, a health and armor bar, a picture of your avatar's head (visually showing what kind of physical state you are in), and a keycard indicator. Above this, you can see a hand holding a variety of weapons. You can move about horizontally (including strafing),[1] look freely around,[2] use a generic action key to open doors and press buttons, collect objects such as health kits and ammo and armor lying around the place, and shoot—there's lots of shooting. In academic terms, *DOOM* is based around the core activity of lining up objects with the center of the screen and removing them by pressing the shoot button. You start in a complex environment, and you simplify it by removing agents and pressing all the buttons there are to press and collecting all the objects there are to collect. You can cut part of the simplification process out by just running for the exit (normally impossible without first finding a keycard or two), but although this is possible—and we'll return to speedruns in subsequent chapters—the game is all about simplifying the environment, with extreme prejudice.

DOOM takes place in an industrial base on a Martian moon that has been invaded by demons from Hell. You are the last survivor, and gameplay takes the form of you battling onward through a variety of locations, exterminating anything that moves. The demons are intent on reducing you to a bloody smear on the corporate carpet, and attempt to do so by clawing, biting, and rending you at close range and by blasting you with shotguns and fireballs from a distance. If you haven't played *DOOM* but have played any first-person shooter, you already know this is fast, simple gameplay, alternating between tense exploration and adrenaline-fueled gunfights. If you haven't played either *DOOM* or any other FPS, your life is poorer as a result, and you should stop reading this and get in on the action immediately. That's the basic overview; we'll go into more detail later on, but from here on in, I'm going to assume you have, at the least, an awareness of a product called *DOOM* out there in the world and some inkling of what playing it entails.

The first release of *DOOM* occurred on December 10, 1993, in the form of a free shareware episode available for download, plus two further episodes requiring payment. The fact that id used the embryonic Internet as a distribution channel, co-opting the emerging online communities, speaks volumes about just how cleverly they understood the context into which their game was going to launch. Netscape was founded in October 1994, the Mosaic web browser (National Center for Supercomputing Applications) in January 1993. These were the glory days of the Gopher protocol, computerized bulletin board systems, and Usenet. Networked games were not necessarily new. MUSE had launched *MUD1* via CompuServe and Compu-Net in the United States and the United Kingdom in 1985, and the ancient equivalent of LAN battles had actually been hardwired into the genre from its very conception, with networked games being established through the 1970s. The idea of using modem-to-modem networks to support multiplay globally was a hugely ambitious goal. Bear in mind, this is all before Steam and other online game stores, way before any general idea of mass digital distribution of games was in the offing. Users were used to file sharing, of course, but the idea of inviting mass, user-driven distribution of a full third of a game as a marketing exercise was quite brilliant, and as we shall see, id co-opted Scott Miller's brilliance to propel *DOOM* sales sky-high.

It's next to impossible to accurately capture sales data for *DOOM* (for reasons we will explore later on), let alone figures for the shareware distribution. Kushner estimates that orders amounting to $100,000 a day hit id in the days just after release (Kushner 2003). In the 2000 edition of *The Complete Wargames Handbook,* combined sales for *DOOM* and *Ultimate DOOM* (version 1.9, released in 1995 and the first traditional retail release) from 1993 to 2000 come in at over 1.8 million units (Dunnigan 2000, 8). VGChartz gives a total figure of 2.85 million as of 2011.[3] Regardless of the impossibility of verification, the fact that community sites claim over ten million installations by 1995 gives some sense, at least, of what a phenomenon it was.[4]

DOOM was an instant, if controversial, critical smash. While players lapped it up, some form of media backlash was pretty inevitable, and the game was attacked for its graphic violence and content. This may look faintly ridiculous now, in the era of *Manhunt* (Rockstar North 2007), *[PROTOTYPE]* (Radical 2009), and *Saw: The Videogame* (Zombie Studios 2009) (let alone the *Saw* movie franchise), but anti-*DOOM* hysteria bubbled into the press with all the vigor of ichor bubbling up from a shotgunned Imp's neck stump. David Grossman famously described it as a "mass murder simulator" (*60 Minutes,* CBS, 1997), and the game was at the center of attempts to push through compulsory licensing of virtual realities. This was driven up to fever pitch with the disclosure that Eric Harris, one of the Columbine shooters, was a keen *DOOM* player and had created his own mods—both of which were linked directly to the shooting by the *Rocky Mountain News* (August 22, 1999), among others. Rumors even circulated that Harris had modded Columbine levels. Regardless of the truth or fiction of media stories, one thing is certain: controversy sells. The hype and the horror stories catapulted *DOOM* even further into the public sphere. Perhaps as much because of this reception as because of how efficiently the content works in a ludic setting, hell, industrial sci-fi, conspiracies involving military-industrial complexes, and shooters were fused together, and this combination still represents the spine of the overwhelming majority of FPS content.

But *DOOM* is not just about the game itself. Pumping away within the shattered rib cage of the Phobos Anomaly was an engine that broke new ground technologically and sat at the top of one of the first true engine dynasties. It's not just the case of id finding a gameplay model that worked for them with *Wolfenstein 3D*, via *Catacomb 3D* (id Software 1991), and then refining this for *DOOM*; it's about coding solutions. From texture mapping to lighting, id took the current boundaries of game technology and drove them forward. It wasn't so much that *DOOM* did things that no one had done before. *Ultima Underworld* (Blue Sky Productions 1992) let the user freely look around using the mouse and pushed the envelope on texture mapping, for example, but *DOOM* pushed these capabilities further and married them to fast, seamless, responsive gameplay. It had everything that was developing in the first-person RPG scene, but it stripped back the complexity of the gameplay and shoved everything into performance. The result was a Formula One car of a game, next to *Ultima*'s camper van. It may not have been complicated or diverse and may not have offered such a range of customization, characterization, story, affordances, and dramatic range, but it was fast. It stands as a brilliant exercise in engine optimization—or gameplay optimization, depending on your stance—with everything serving an experience that shoved the player through an affective pipe at a breakneck pace, only letting up on them to replace action with tension and a pause to admire the scenery. *DOOM* was built for speed.

One last thing: If you haven't played *DOOM* in a while, hunt down and dust off your copy. You know it's lurking around somewhere, hissing like a Cacodemon. Play it all over again. Because it's just, quite simply, a really bloody good game.

CHAPTER 1

Eva! Auf Wiedersehen!

The Birth of a Genre

We need to consider the context into which *DOOM* arrived. The very first FPS game was *Maze War,* created by Steve Colley, Howard Palmer, and Greg Thompson (and other contributors) at the NASA Ames Research Center. Colley estimates that the first version was built during 1973,[1] as an extension of the earlier game *Maze,* which offered a first-person exploration of a basic wireframe environment. At some point during '73 or '74, networked capability was added, enabling multiplayer FPS play. The genre was born out of networked deathmatching. After Thompson moved to MIT, he continued to develop *Maze War,* adding a server offering personalized games, increasing the number of players to eight, and adding simple bots to the mix. Twenty years before *DOOM,* all of the prototypical features of the FPS were in place: a 3D real-time environment, simple ludic activity (look, move, shoot, take damage), and a basic set of goals and win/lose conditions—all this and multiplayer networked combat.

Around the same time, Jim Bowery developed *Spasim* (1974), which he has claimed to be the very first 3D networked multiplayer game.[2] *Spasim* pitted up to thirty-two players (eight players in four planetary systems) against one another over a network, with each taking control of a space ship, viewed to other players as a wireframe. A second version expanded the gameplay from simple combat to include resource management and more strategic elements. Whether or not Bowery's argument that *Spasim* precurses *Maze War* and represents the first FPS holds water, its importance as a game is undiminished—even if for no other reason than because *Spa-*

sim is a clear spiritual ancestor of *Elite* (Braben and Bell 1984) and its many derivatives. It perhaps even prototypes a game concept that would later spin out into combat-oriented real-time strategy (RTS) or even massively multiplayer online (MMO) gaming.

What certainly differentiates *Spasim* from *Maze War* is the perspective. Like other early first-person games, such as *BattleZone* (Atari 1980) and id's *Hovertank 3D* (1991), the game is essentially vehicular, with no representation of the avatar onscreen other than a crosshair. It is interesting that, aside from occasional titles such as *Descent* (Parallax 1995) and *Forsaken* (Probe Entertainment 1998), the genre very swiftly settled down into the avatar-based perspective, abandoning vehicular combat more or less completely. It's also interesting that contemporary shooters often opt for a shift to third-person when including vehicles, such as with *Halo: Combat Evolved* (Bungie 2002) or *Rage* (id Software 2011). *Half-Life 2*'s (Valve Software 2004) first-person car sequences are actually quite unusual.

In 1992, Blue Sky Productions released *DOOM*'s calmer, more reasonable sibling, a first-person role-playing game called *Ultima Underworld: The Stygian Abyss*. The *Ultima* RPG series had been around since 1981 and was already part of a tradition opting for first-person perspective in a much more complex game. *Akalabeth* (Richard Garriott 1980) used wireframe graphics, in the manner of *Maze War,* alternated with top-down gameplay. This style became more prevalent as games shifted to tiled graphics, but the inclusion of first-person perspective remained constant (e.g., through the embedded window in Sir-Tech's *Wizardry* series or Jagware's 1986 *Alien Fires: 2199 AD*). RPGs began to return to first-person in greater numbers as the technology caught up with the aspirations of early titles. *Dungeon Master* (FTL Games 1987) leapt the genre forward in terms of real-time 3D action, and others soon followed. What marks these games out, however, is the retention of predominantly RPG-flavored gameplay, based on complex controls, resource gathering, and stat management. *Ultima Underworld* broke new ground in the responsiveness of controls, the degrees of perceptual freedom and movement, and a renewed emphasis for combat in real time. If it wasn't for the fact that an upstart little company called id had released their own first-person dungeon crawler, featuring radically stripped-back gameplay and a push toward frantic, fast-paced action that made *Stygian Abyss* feel positively sluggish by comparison, *Ultima* would be in a strong position to claim rights to igniting the modern FPS powder keg. As is, the debts owed by RPG/FPS crossovers from *Deus Ex* (Ion

Storm 2000) to *Borderlands* (Gearbox 2009) and *Fallout 3* (Bethesda 2008) are clear, and while less explicit, most FPS games of anything other than the most basic twitch shooters trace their genealogy back to somewhere in the *Ultima* family. But *Catacomb 3D* (id Software 1991) was different (fig. 1). It was bloody. It was basic. It was fast. It was fun.

Catacomb started out as a 2D shooter with an RPG-flavored world in 1989 and went through a couple of variations before it went 3D in 1991. The template for *DOOM* is set here. The representation of the avatar is limited to the form of a hand at the bottom of the screen. There's a familiar heads-up display (HUD), which really didn't evolve that much between the two titles. There are multiple means of attacking enemies (basic fireball, stream of fireballs, and a short-range area effect centered on the avatar) and an evolving succession of fantasy enemies to fight. This all takes place in a maze that the player progresses through using required colored keys, normally found by identifying and destroying secret passages in weakened wall sections. *Catacomb 3D*'s story was pure RPG hack and more or less completely superfluous to the action. While id has never really invested that much in its plots, we can see with both *Wolfenstein 3D* and *DOOM* that even if you don't really care about story, setting is a powerful tool in game design. In *Catacomb 3D*, the player explores a series of more or less identikit fantasy settings: a graveyard, a mausoleum, a garden, all of which use a basic set of square wall textures and occasional props in the exploratory space to distinguish between them. Agents are preplaced in the maze and do not respawn once an area is cleared. Critically, although *Catacomb 3D*'s world is straightforward Dungeons & Dragons guff, the gameplay itself has nothing to do with RPGs, the odd obsessive fan aside. Configuration is completely abandoned. The player starts with access to three combat abilities. New areas are exposed by shooting away walls that are visually (and textually) announced to be different (weak). You can pick up treasure, health, or potions (the equivalent of ammo). There is practically no avatar representation, characterization, or development. This is an arcade game bolted onto an RPG-styled HUD and world. John Romero comments,

> When we made *Catacomb 3D*, the game didn't feel as cool as it should—it was very interesting in its technology and what we were trying to do. . . . At the same time we released *Commander Keen*, which was way more fun than *Catacomb 3D*, but [*Catacomb 3D*] looked like it had a direction, a promise we could go after. (JR)[3]

The Mausoleum of Nemesis

THE CATACOMB ABYSS

©1992 SOFTDISK INC

100%

Item destroyed

Fig 1. *Catacomb 3D*

The follow-up to *Catacomb 3D* discarded any notion of the RPG. Whereas *Catacomb 3D* could potentially be described (if you really wanted to) as an arcade-style RPG-lite game, *Wolfenstein 3D,* released as shareware on May 5, 1992, is a shooter, pure and simple. Goodbye ghouls, healing potions, and crypts. Hello chainguns, pseudo-supernaturalized sci-fi, and, most important, blasting Nazis. *Wolfenstein 3D* not only offered a radical break from the normal deployment of first-person perspective in gaming; it stalked the RPG through the corridors of the medium, blasted it at short-range with a shotgun, and planted a flag in the sucking chest wound of the corpse. The FPS had arrived. Romero recalls,

> On the home computer, we had a major drought of any fast play . . . because everything on the computer had to go through CPUs, so the PC had all these plodding, turn-based titles. . . . So when we were making *Wolfenstein 3D,* getting rid of anything that slowed it down made it feel truer to the arcade skill that we were used to. (JR)

Wolfenstein 3D was loosely based on the side-scrolling arcade game *Wolfenstein,* created by Silas Warner in 1981. Taking the basic premise of escape from a Nazi castle, id dispensed largely with the stealth approach that formed much of the gameplay of Warner's game. Rather than encouraging the player to avoid detection, *Wolfenstein 3D* is a straightforward shooter. Environments are simple and clean, with level-to-level progression based around finding the elevator to the next floor, which usually requires the player to find at least one key to get through locked doors. There are no variations in room heights, and textures are only applied to walls. This is simpler than the environments offered by *Ultima Underworld,* but the compromise enabled the game to run at a greater speed, effectively sacrificing complexity for performance. Likewise, *Wolfenstein 3D* offers fewer agents, with very simple behavior. It is possible to sneak up on soldiers, for example, but the core gameplay is fast, furious, bloody. Romero's vision was clear.

> Originally *Wolfenstein 3D* had all that—dragging bodies, picking locks. But when we started playing it, we figured . . . what use is there in trying to hide stuff or drag it round when all I'm doing is just blowing stuff up anyway? So let's get rid of all of the things that stop us in our tracks and pretty much force the player to just mow everything down—just make the player destroy stuff constantly. (JR)

Treasure is available for *Wolfenstein 3D* players to collect, the HUD features a score counter (dispensed with in *DOOM*), and there are secret areas leading to ammo, health, and treasure. But exploration is really only there for completionist players, rather than being essential or even particularly advantageous.

Wolfenstein 3D is split into six episodes, each comprised of ten levels. The story is an exercise in brutal simplicity. In the first episode, B. J. Blazkowicz, an allied spy, must escape from a Nazi stronghold. The player fights through the prison, eventually reaching the final boss, Hans Grosse. Episode two sees Blazkowicz return to stop a new biological warfare threat, represented by zombie agents with machine guns implanted in their chests and a syringe-hurling boss, Dr. Schabbs. The final episode culminates with a battle with Adolf Hitler, complete with robot exoskeleton, in the bunker beneath the Reichstag. The second batch of three episodes involves further chemical war shenanigans but is largely indistinguishable from the first, and to be fair, a player looking for fulfillment in *Wolfenstein 3D*'s story is probably going to miss the point and would likely get a more engaging experience reading the back of a cigarette packet. There's little going on apart from a very basic exercise in scene setting and establishing a premise: shoot as many Nazis as possible while running about a series of similar-looking environments, collecting treasure as you go (if that's your thing).

The *Wolfenstein 3D* player has access to only four weapons: a knife, a pistol, a machine gun, and a chaingun. There is a single health counter that can be topped up with health kits, stolen Nazi dinners, and dog food. There is a limited range of objects—tables, torture gibbets, and green barrels (not exploding yet, we had to wait until *DOOM* for that). The secret areas in the levels are rarely signposted, so for every door lurking behind a portrait of Hitler, there are two triggered by attempting to open otherwise indistinguishable walls. The lack of dynamic lighting and the basic texture set means that progress through the levels is often a result of trial and error and of exhausting the environment using a trail of bodies to work out where you have previously been. While it's important not to be overly critical of *Wolfenstein 3D*'s simplicity or lack of signposting, it does demonstrate how the technological advances of *DOOM* suddenly threw such devices into general usage.

Wolfenstein 3D was a critical and commercial success. It won the People's Choice and Best Entertainment Software categories at the 1993 Shareware Industry Awards, Best Arcade Game from *Compute!* (1992), Most Innovative Game and Best Action Game from *Videogames and Computer Entertainment* (1992), the Reader's Choice—Action/Arcade Game award from *Game Bytes* (1992), and Best Action Game from *Computer Gaming World* (1993). It was ported to Mac, Acorn, the Super Nintendo Entertainment System, Game Boy, Jaguar, and others, still enjoying life on contemporary platforms such as iPhone and PlayStation 3. A follow-up, *Spear of Destiny,* released later in 1992 by id, carried on the rich tradition of pure Nazi hokum and tongue-in-cheek graphic violence. The series was reinvented by Gray Matter Interactive in 2001. Less frantic than the original, *Return to Castle Wolfenstein* placed more emphasis on story and exploration and diversified the gameplay, as might be expected of a development in the post-*Quake* (id Software 1996), post-*Half-Life* era. Nerve Software developed the multiplayer aspect of the game, and this was then spun off into *Enemy Territory* (Splash Damage 2003), a free multiplayer-only game. In 2009, id collaborated with Raven Software and Pi Studios to release *Wolfenstein,* a reboot that added the equivalent of magic powers and upgrades to the expected mix of supernatural cyborg Nazis. It was generally favorably received, with many critics noting that, it delivered in terms of competent gameplay what it lacked in inspiration or originality. It also proved that blasting undead Nazis had lost none of its charm in the seventeen-year interim.

To understand *DOOM,* you really have to understand *Wolfenstein 3D* and the seeds that were planted within its development. In essence, *Wolfenstein 3D* established a set of conceptual design constraints, in its refusal to be counted alongside games like *Ultima Underworld. DOOM* might add complexity in the form of lighting, shifting environments with a vastly bigger range of textures, switches and lifts, and a bevy of demonic enemies to battle, but *Wolfenstein 3D* set the ground rules. This was 3D arcade gaming without compromise. Everything else was disposable. A conflict around this lack of compromise set the ground for id's first major split and, arguably, its transition into a grown-up company.

CHAPTER 2

The Speed of Light Sucks

The Rise of id

The meteoric rise of id Software is the stuff of gaming legend, a larger-than-life tale of ambition, ego, and raw talent. In what is likely to remain the definitive book on early id, *Masters of DOOM: How Two Guys Created an Empire and Transformed Pop Culture,* Kushner (2003) argues that what ultimately catapulted id to fame was the collision of two exceptional talents—John Carmack and John Romero—coming together at a hinge point in the development of gaming as a medium. Without underplaying the equally exceptional supporting cast (Adrian Carmack, Tom Hall, Kevin Cloud, Sandy Peterson, Jay Wilbur,[1] and a host of others), Kushner clearly sees Carmack and Romero as the Lennon and McCartney of gaming. Maybe comparing them to Johnny Rotten and Sid Vicious would be more appropriate, only without a Malcolm McLaren operating behind the scenes. If the story of id can be read as the American dream in action and then a cautionary tale of its implosion, it's also straight out of punk, pure and simple.[2]

I'm not going to rehash chunks of Kushner's book here. It's a really great book and very readable, and you should probably hop across to it straight after this if your interest in id has been sparked. I'm going to keep us focused here on the frothing petri dish that spawned the monster. What follows is a brief, potted history on who made *DOOM* and why. It's important to note that not everyone agrees with Kushner's emphasis on the two figureheads at id. Todd Hollenshead, now CEO at id, thinks reducing the *DOOM* team to the two most visible members doesn't do justice to the spread of input and talent across the studio. In particular, he singles out Adrian Carmack's art as being underrepresented when *DOOM* is talked about.

> Adrian is a supremely talented natural artist who never got enough public credit back in the day for the work he put in on *DOOM* and *DOOM II*. If I can speak to his contribution, it's his imagination that created basically all of the demons in *DOOM*. He was quoted once as saying, "I have nightmares and then draw them," which is probably not far from what really happened. The story has been told over and over that it was John Carmack and John Romero that created all the old games, with Carmack being the technical genius and Romero being the game designer. That makes a good story, but that's not how I see it. First of all, those games were developed by the whole team, with everyone making substantial contributions. Crediting just two people on the team with the majority of the work is misleading. John Carmack's tech was and remains amazing, but it is gated by the quality of the art. It was the imagination of Adrian Carmack that brought it all to life. (THo)[3]

The id story begins at SoftDisk, a subscription company that first rolled out its monthly disc for Apple II computers back in 1981. Romero joined the company in 1989, after an abortive start-up venture seduced him away from Origin, his first major professional role. After a period making games to be released on the standard SoftDisk monthlies, Romero, along with Jay Wilbur, convinced the company to create a specialist game disc, *Gamer's Edge*. The *Gamer's Edge* group recruited a programmer named John Carmack, who was already creating waves in the gaming scene, and Adrian Carmack, who was an intern at SoftDisk at that point. The group also roped in Tom Hall, although he didn't officially join the team at first. The core team of id Software came together and, in the face of a relatively unenthusiastic SoftDisk, began to hatch their plans for world domination. The major breakthrough, according to Kushner, came when John Carmack managed to re-create Nintendo's console side-scrolling on the PC, in a prototype aptly titled *Dangerous Dave in Copyright Infringement*. Romero was quick to see the huge potential for this and for PC gaming to break out of the rut of slow-moving, strategy- or adventure-based titles, reclaiming a more arcade-styled territory from the burgeoning console market (although the team did send a PC port of *Super Mario Bros. 3* [1988] to Nintendo, who declined to pick it up). When SoftDisk failed to live up to the ambitions of the team members, they decided that they were going to go it alone, if with a little "help" from SoftDisk. In real terms, this meant "borrowing" computers from the office outside working hours and hiding their developments from the rest of the company. The game became *Commander Keen* (1990), and was released as a trilogy, the first part of which went out as shareware (the model also used for *Wolfenstein 3D* and *DOOM*). Keen was a hit, starting a relationship with Scott Miller's Apogee and signaling the end of employment with SoftDisk, which, despite being less than impressed with being the unwitting hosts for id's embryonic phase, recognized the potential of the team that were calling themselves "Ideas from the Deep" and tried to cut a deal with them. It failed, and "Ideas from the Deep" was shortened to "In Demand" and finally "id."[4]

id Software was officially formed in 1991 and released *Hovertank 3D* the same year, alongside fulfilling some outstanding contractual requirements for SoftDisk. In *Hovertank 3D,* we can see the development of both technology and design toward the gameplay and aesthetics of *Wolfenstein 3D* and *DOOM.* There are no textures (just block colors), progress through the game is much more sluggish compared to the later titles, and the gameplay is as much about rescuing hostages as blasting bad guys; but the groundwork was being laid.

Perhaps what defines early id more than anything else was a singularity of vision and ambition that still leaves most games companies standing in the dust. Historically, of course, the partnership of Carmack and Romero fractured messily and publicly, although whether this was due to a breakdown in shared vision or the pressures of a sudden catapulting into celebrity is open to some discussion. The first tension, however, centered on Tom Hall, who was primarily responsible for the vision of the *Keen* series and voiced unease about the direction in which the new game in development, *Wolfenstein 3D*, was headed. Quite simply, the breakthroughs in technology being driven by John Carmack were creating potential for Adrian Carmack to explore a darker, bloodier stream of consciousness. At the same time, Hall remained committed to fusing arcade action with more complex stories, something that marginalized him in the face of the highly simplified, cartoon content that other members of the team were pushing toward. Following *Wolfenstein 3D*, Hall was anxious that *DOOM* should have something resembling a story. He contended that there was no reason why the gameplay could not be fused with more complex diegetic content. The *DOOM* Bible, which is discussed in the next chapter, clearly shows this vision beginning to emerge. However, it did not fall into line with the singular thrust of the rest of id's vision. Despite continuing to work on *DOOM*'s early development, Hall resigned in 1993. The vacuum was filled by Sandy Petersen, the creator of the paper-based RPG *Call of Cthulhu* (Chaosium 1981), a man for whom gothic, hellish worlds and their denizens were a staple diet. Peterson and Romero took on the core responsibility for the level design on *DOOM* (including working from some of Hall's drafts). Bobby Prince, the audio designer for *Wolfenstein 3D*, returned, bringing to the project a thumping metal soundtrack that, in its own way, has left a legacy to game audio that has been as influential as *DOOM*'s technical or visual legacy.

There's no doubt about the fact that id, particularly Romero and Carmack, became true rock stars of gaming. After *DOOM* became an overnight sensation (again, there's no hyperbole in that), the studio parking lot was packed with high-performance sports cars. Romero, in particular, was not just famous for designing *DOOM*; he became a real figurehead, the Big Daddy of Deathmatch and the public face of the company. While Carmack retreated back into pushing the next wave of technology forward, Romero very publicly lived the celebrity high life, as high profile a gamer as he was a developer. During the buildup to and release of *DOOM II*, Carmack was already working on the *Quake* engine, and tension was beginning to build in the company. American McGee was recruited as a level designer, joining Petersen. *Quake* was beset by delays and technical issues, and Romero was increasingly blamed for a lack of direction in the team. In particular, the uneasy mix of fantasy and sci-fi in *Quake*, which could, not entirely unfairly, be caricatured as more of a tech demo than a game, may have been rooted in the ongoing splintering of vision at the heart of id, manifesting in the disparate and somewhat clumsy mix of levels presented in the game. *Quake*'s story, such as it is, feels like a halfhearted bolt-on, an attempt to cover up the lack of cohesion in the final product.[5] Technologically, *Quake* is a marvel, but in terms of gameplay and aesthetics, it doesn't really have the fine-toothed balance that made *DOOM* such an outstanding achievement—although I'm perfectly happy to accept that a vast army of fans will probably disagree with me there. Either way, the struggle to make *Quake* left an unbridgeable schism at the heart of id, and Romero, facing an ultimatum from the other owners, resigned on August 6, 1996.

What happened next is outside the scope of this book, but in terms of putting *DOOM* in context, the preceding account should start to paint a picture of the organizational mentality, the unique hive mind, that spawned *DOOM*. First, a major thing to draw from this account is best summed up by Romero:

> I grew up in the arcades, and so naturally I wanted the arcades on the computer. And John did too, so our natural instinct was always to make things as fast as we could make them, to mimic the arcades. (JR)

Although both Carmack and Romero had been programming games for PC for some time, this drive to get back to the arcades permeates the decisions made building up to *DOOM*. The speed of *Wolfenstein 3D* was a radical departure from contemporary PC gaming, and to embed this sense of pace into a game as detailed and dynamic as *DOOM* was a major factor in making the game stand out. Second, id was a small, fast, hugely ambitious company of people who were as uncompromising as they were obsessed with games and game technology and with a vision of where these might be headed. The old adage of not making an omelet without breaking a few eggs is particularly apt to the early years of this company. Third, calling id "punk" (i.e., a rebellious counterculture group) is not just a sound bite but a really quite accurate metaphor of the way the company thought and worked (although the personal musical tastes ran more toward metal). id was put together in a back room of a larger company, fighting against perceived lack of vision and ambition, with little desire to kowtow to received wisdom or commercial pressure. This wasn't just a snotty refusal but was underpinned by a profoundly perceptive understanding of the new opportunities opened up by bulletin board systems and other networking technologies. Equally, like the best punk bands, id's games may have sounded simple on the surface, but beneath the high-speed two and a half minutes of noise, there was a very deep and serious understanding of the medium and the technology. In other words, the members of the id team might have been making an unholy noise, but they could *really* play their instruments. They just chose to turn their backs on prog. Fourth (and closely related to the third point), the team was made up of gamers, through and through, and based both design and business decisions on staying true to a culture they still felt very much a part of. Romero's well-documented love of his own games is not just luck, ego, or a result of living the development dream; it drove the types of games id made. While this is true of all developers to one extent or another, it's this instinct that arguably led to the multiplayer sections of *DOOM* becoming as important as they did. What's more fun than arcade games? Competitive arcade games! What makes tabletop RPGs and battle gaming so much fun? In part, it has to be the unpredictability of other people, the fact that they learn, experiment, shift tactics, and try to outsmart you in a way that artificial intelligence at that time just couldn't get close to. And there's the pure, simple fun of fragging a friend. I look forward greatly to the days when the sound of Romeroesque bellows of "Eat death, shitmonkey!" echo around the corridors of retirement homes and when octogenerian deathmatchers show the young whippersnappers a thing or two about rocket jumping. That's quite a legacy. Finally, in an era where extensive market research, playtesting, and publisher pressure are only, largely thanks to the rise of the indie scene, starting to lose their grip on creativity in game design, *DOOM* still feels very much like a gamer's game. It retains the edge of old-school bedroom development, as idiosyncratic and uncompromising as *Llamatron* (Llamasoft 1991) or *Elite*.

A few other things leading to *DOOM* should be mentioned. Hall, from early on in the Keen trilogy, was interested in representing the consequences of the player's actions. The shift in graphical quality made it possible to show the player what shooting might do, in a heavily reduced, stylized way of course. It's interesting that what ended up as brains popping out in a cartoon spray in *DOOM* actually started with the notion of a moral imperative, ironic given *DOOM*'s supposedly demonic influence on teen violence and desensitization. Equally, the fact that id shifted quickly from *Hovertank 3D* to *Catacomb 3D*—from vehicular HUD to avatar HUD—is worth noting. John Carmack ties this in to the rhetoric and expectations of virtual reality that were very much part of the landscape at the time. In fact, he argues that the virtual reality (VR) scene offers an important contextual backdrop for understanding some of the development decisions that went into the process of refining the 3D engines from *Hovertank 3D* to *Catacomb 3D* to *Wolfenstein 3D*.

> And all the while we were doing *DOOM,* there was all the talk about VR as a high concept. . . . I mean, there were already flight simulators out there, and people were talking about virtual reality, touchy-feely, Jaron Lanier, that sort of stuff. . . . But it isn't exactly clear that people would have taken 3D out of the simulationy slow-based world and turned it into this action stuff in the near-term that we wound up doing that in. That probably was the key contribution of the whole *Wolfenstein 3D, DOOM,*

Quake legacy, is making it work on a very fast-paced, adrenaline-fueled action game, when 3D was restricted to these much more sedate simulation, almost academic interest things. Of course, that's all games are: you're going in there, you're interacting with a simulation at some level, but it's not necessarily a simulation of reality. . . .

But the thing that hooked people, that got them in there, was that it was really the first time in gaming you had the ability to project yourself into this world. You know, when somebody got surprised by something in a traditional arcade game, they could be sweating and intense about it, but you'd be like "Dammit, you lost!" But in a first-person game, when you turn around a corner and there's something you didn't expect, especially in the early days before people became somewhat inured to it, we had people literally falling out of their seats. You don't get this from any other style of game, and that's when we knew we were pushing on something a little bit different. (JC)[6]

CHAPTER 3

Beefy Chunklets from Bible to Beta

At the beginning of *DOOM*'s development, Tom Hall created a document to collect his thoughts and inform the design process. The *DOOM* Bible[1] contains some basic design information such as endgame states, command-line prompts, lists of graphics and audio, and, at the end, press releases, a glossary of terms, information on extensions and utilities, and the phone numbers and addresses of local fast-food delivery outlets. The central section is taken up with what proved to be the flash point of Hall and id's split: the story.

In fact, both Hall and Romero agree that the final version of the game doesn't actually deviate that much from Hall's original vision. For Romero, this is because the Bible establishes the world of the game—a concept, some leads on environments, ideas for weapons, all generic world-building details. What didn't make it, he suggests are "some things that were just too one-offish and didn't add to the experience" (JR). The most notable of these casualties are the five characters of the original concept. What's important about this is that as far as the Bible seems to be concerned, *DOOM* was envisaged as a multiplayer co-op. Once again, this shows just how far ahead of the curve the members of the id team were thinking in terms of the FPS. During the first episode, designed to be released as shareware, the action returns to the room seen in the opening cutscenes, where a card game is interrupted by the invasion. The Bible states that it contains "four minus the number of players' bodies."

After the emphasis on cooperative play, the second major deviation is in the complexity of the story and its episodic structure. Although the basic story of *DOOM* actually made it into the released game—albeit spread across both *DOOM* and *DOOM II* (id Software 1995)—Hall's original story involves multiple battles around multiple dimensional gates. The initial crisis remains the same, as does the player entering a gate at the end of Episode 1 and fighting through Hell to return. At this point, *DOOM* concludes, but the Bible story has much more to give. The player returns to find another base, also overrun, and beats off the demon threat there. Episode 3 ends with the entire moon being bombed, destroying the dimensional gate. The action then shifts to another moon; Episodes 4 and 5 describe an assault on this moon and the attempt to reclaim a stolen weapon (with a tour of Hell thrown in). Finally, Episode 6 introduces a third gate location and the need to destroy a demonic machine that is enlarging the small rift, before more forces can come through. At this point, the Bible shifts to "Commercial Game," which sees the invasion of Earth by demonic forces. As Hall puts it, "My *DOOM* Bible detailed a progression from Earth to Hell to Earth-corrupted-by-Hell, which is the most disturbing. . . . And that's funny since they did finish that arc in *DOOM II*" (THa).[2]

There is no doubt that the final version of *DOOM* simplified this structure considerably, reducing it to the attempted escape from Phobos, the assault on Deimos, and the battle through Hell, returning to an Earth already invaded in the final, postplay plot twist. The cutscenes, multiple characters, complex narrative, and action that spans multiple worlds are all gone. This ties in with Romero's insistence that the Bible essentially acted as a world-prompting tool rather than a narrative structure, and the core aspect of it was the central idea of fusing science fiction with supernatural horror.

> The Bible wasn't too specific about design stuff. It was like here are locations, here's the idea if this anomaly happens, and instead of aliens from somewhere in the universe coming through, it's demons from hell, which is a total juxtaposition from what you expect to see in space. You'd never expect that in space, and that was our cool hook, that something you'd just never expect. (JR)

Famously, this now recurring theme in gaming came about through id's off-duty role playing. John Carmack (as Dungeon Master, of course) had created a complex world containing a powerful magic book controlling the demonic realms. Romero, in return for personally gaining an equally powerful weapon, the Daikatana, gave it to the leader of the demons, allowing them to overrun and destroy the world. The second major influence was James Cameron's film *Aliens* (1986). Kushner reports that Jay Wilbur, then working as id's business manager, investigated purchasing the rights for making a game of the movie but that the team decided against it: "They didn't want some movie company telling them what they could and couldn't put in their game" (2003, 122). But as Romero puts it, id loved not only the setting of *Aliens* but also "the fear and the speed of it" (JR). A third influence was Sam Raimi's film *The Evil Dead* (1981), which brought black, gross-out humor and a chainsaw to the party. From this basic premise, this fusion of worlds and styles, Hall constructed his story, and although he agrees with Romero that the Bible saturates the game in terms of concepts and design ideas, he maintains that abandoning basically all characters and all but the most basic plot was unnecessary.

> All I wanted for *DOOM* is that little bit of start story to give meaning to what you are doing. For example, *Aliens* would have been a good movie if they landed and aliens jumped out and were scary. But there were two bits of story—worry about the missing child Newt and seeing all the alien transponders in one place. So you were pulled forward by one and afraid of facing the other but knew Ripley had to go there. So that deepens the tension and emotion, and you are invested in it. And that for *DOOM* could've been easy and simple. Of course, it's brilliant as it is though. (THa)

The Bible only goes into detail about Episode 1. There are fifteen environments described, each including subareas, special features, and Easter eggs. Without doubt, Hall was aiming for a more "realistic" pathway through the base, and this was evident in his early level designs. Along with the complex story, this push for realism was abandoned in favor of high-impact, more comic-book stylings. After Petersen was drafted in, he rebuilt several of Hall's levels, adding the more lurid, gothic elements for which his levels are notable. In fact, Romero sees much of the final design, the final feel of the game, as a product of the process of actually building it, reaffirming the Bible's status as conceptual primer, rather than design document. As will be discussed in the next chapter, as *DOOM* was developing as a game, so Carmack and Romero were breaking new ground technologically, and these advances created the design space as much as they were solutions to design problems. According to Romero, the early work on *DOOM* did little more than clone *Wolfenstein 3D*, as can be seen in the earliest tech preview,

released on February 4, 1993. While the members of the id team were committed to a new vision, a new game that leapt forward from *Wolfenstein 3D*,
they were still working on the older tool set, creating new applications as
they needed them. The Bible describes several of these: Lumpy, WadLink,
and the Fuzzy Pumper Palette Shop.[3] But it also lists the new features being
worked toward: Carmack's texture mapping, nonorthogonal walls, variable
heights, new light sourcing and illumination drop-offs, and palette transitions for increased color use, as well as making much of the multiplayer
dimension and environment morphing, which perhaps didn't really come
into its own until *Quake*. The Bible also includes the immortal line "In 1993,
we fully expect to be the number one cause of decreased productivity in
businesses around the world." I will return to this in chapter 7. Of course,
not all of these tools and functions were available at the outset (far from it),
and id's heady ambitions for both game design and game technology pour
out of the Bible like Imps from a dimensional portal.

Given the height of the bar the members of the id team had very publically set themselves, it's no surprise that early design was a challenge.
Romero sees this as a mental, conceptual challenge as much as anything
else, a need to "break out of that design space we were in from *Wolfenstein
3D*." There is little doubt that his ethos of designing from the player's perspective, a natural sense of what he would want to see in the game, provided
momentum to the breaking out of *Wolfenstein 3D* and into *DOOM*. He recalls,

> So I told the artist that I'm going to go and figure this out right now;
> I'm not going to wait for anybody to define what *DOOM* is going to
> look like, I'm doing it now. So I went in my office, taking a break from
> programming DoomEd, . . . spent a while coming up with an interest-
> ing little flow area, you know, a pathway, going up some stairs. And the
> pathway was kind of claustrophobic, with varying light levels and stairs,
> and then it opens up into this giant room, and then there were raised
> areas on the sides of this, with monsters, and that was actually a room
> that ended up being in E1M2,[4] the second level of the game—it's still in
> there. But that one room was something I thought looked really cool,
> and when I got the artist to look at it, I just said, "OK, here you are,"
> and I walked through it, and when we got to that room and it opened
> up, they were like "Yeah, that's awesome" and I thought, "This is it, this
> is how we're doing our levels." So that really defined how we were going

to build our levels, and the whole game reflected that, that level design breakthrough. (JR)

Romero's words are a clear illustration of the mind that took the technological advances and the concept document, chewed them over, and spat back out the essential design vision of *DOOM*. Hall has different recollections of the early phases of design, particularly on the subject of the "one big world" described in the Bible. According to Romero and Hall,[5] this was driven by Carmack and eventually foundered on the technical constraints of the time. Hall recalls,

> In *DOOM,* I was flat out against one big world. I thought the players liked the level-to-level nature of *Wolfenstein 3D* and that was wrong to change. But it was decided to do one big world. So I designed that for weeks. Then it was back to level-to-level, overnight, and I'd just wasted tons of work that I disagreed with in the first place. (THa)[6]

Regardless of the extent to which *DOOM* may have been conceptualized as a linear or arena shooter (there are tantalizing hints here of sandboxing, but that may be reading a little too far into things), one thing that the Bible, tech demos, Romero, and Hall all agree on is the need for immersion, realized by carefully crafting a corridor of action, emotional affect, spectacle, and fidelity and then shoving a player down it as fast as ludically and technologically possible. *Immersion* may be a highly problematic word in academic circles, but that hasn't stopped it from being a holy grail for game designers, operating on a populist, fuzzy definition that doesn't appear to give anyone in the industry much cause for concern.[7] A huge amount of *DOOM*'s design is geared toward dragging players into the world and not letting them out again, usually through the easier-said-than-done trick of having them not even consider stopping play. Kevin Cloud talks of the need to engage the player on a level that is more emotional than cognitive.

> You actually *feel* fear where a demon is shooting at you. You play *DOOM* today and it's kind of silly compared to what players are now used to, which is more sophisticated. But back then, with a fireball coming at you, people would physically dodge in their chair, and that was something new to games. (KC)[8]

For both Cloud and Carmack, FPS games were routed as much in the rhetoric of virtual reality as in the history of the arcades. For them, *DOOM* was about challenging the assumptions of virtual reality as proposed by the likes of Jaron Lanier or Howard Rheingold. Interestingly, Cloud argues that the expected future of first-person perspective in games was not necessarily the direction *DOOM* took and that the roots in RPG exerted a great deal of influence.

> From a gameplay perspective, you've got to keep in mind that back then, there were a lot of different directions a first-person game could go. Of course, the first thing that people think about with first-person games is being in a virtual reality, that natural extension: where do I go—what's the eventual extension of a first-person game? It's a holodeck or something. So there was a lot of thinking, OK, this first-person environment would make a great RPG world, kind of dripped in reality, a lot things, very real and detailed. . . . And, of course, with *Wolfenstein 3D* and *DOOM,* we took the idea of just emphasizing combat and having a very fast-paced and visceral and in-your-face action. And that's where the design focus was. (KC)

In *DOOM,* small, tight, cramped, dark corridors suddenly opened into huge expansive spaces; sectors leaked sound into one another, so not only could you hear demons off out there in the dark somewhere, but you could hear them hearing you; and split levels meant that there were places visible but out of reach, begging you to just find the right way. Before you add in the dynamic elements of agents, weapons, and puzzles, the environments of *DOOM* suddenly shifted from *Wolfenstein 3D*'s flat corridors to a world to explore and, critically, one that visually rewarded exploration.

Romero's statement that the game's environments constructed in early 1993 owed more to *Wolfenstein 3D* than to the vision of *DOOM* isn't necessarily true. Without doubt, the February 1993 pre-alpha is fairly basic. It takes the form of a small map with irregular walls in place (i.e., ninety-degree corners have already gone), complete with sprites of three of the demons from the finished game: Hell Knights, Imps, and Pinkys. The fact that these sprites are not only present but remain unchanged right through to the release version suggests, perhaps, that, despite Romero's protestations, there was—at least in part—a singular vision of *DOOM* right there from the start. In a way, the sprites had already evolved way beyond their contemporaries, setting a high bar for the rest of the game to aspire to. The pre-alpha announces itself as "2 months work," but it is already beginning to accelerate away from *Wolfenstein 3D*. It gives the user the option to cycle through a few examples of texture-mapped ceilings, walls, and floors, and although the resolution is low by today's standards, the cartoon flavor of *Wolfenstein 3D* is conspicuously absent. It is clearly apparent that regardless of *DOOM*'s arcade gameplay, the visual identity of the game draws deeply from the first-person RPGs that preceded it, like *Ultima Underworld*.

The other major point of interest in the pre-alpha is the HUD: alongside the weapon indicator, a map is continuously present. The bottom right shows item pickups: a Sandwich, the Heart of Lothian, and the Captain's Hand. At bottom left is a text/speech box. The unique items would be replaced with colored keycards as the progress toward release was made, and this is perhaps one of the most indicative ways in which *DOOM*'s world was streamlined. In fact, the spinning title of the first alpha (April 2, 1993) includes not just credits but high scores, which is about as arcade as it gets and suggests a return to *Wolfenstein 3D*'s treasure chests. Some of the items dotted around as collectables in the alphas—not just ammo and health kits but blood-filled goblets and skull boxes—exist alongside functional items (keycards are also present now) as further evidence that id was toying with a score system. In fact, this is confirmed by the beta press release, which includes an item count in the HUD, alongside counts for health, armor, keycards, and ammo.

The 0_4 alpha version allows the player to explore nine levels, and the distinction between these is telling. It is also the first glimpse of *DOOM* as we know it, particularly levels 1, 4, and 5. Each level starts with the player joined by three other marines; at this point, co-operative multiplay is still very much in the mix. In fact, level 1 actually starts with the card game described in the Bible. A significant proportion of the alpha is at a very early stage: levels are blankly lit and basically textured (fig. 2). Having said that, many of the areas are recycled into the final game, and some parts are instantly recognizable. Nathan Lineback includes on his fan site a full list of which alpha levels ended up integrated into which release levels,[9] and the most obviously recognizable is the fourth alpha level, which became E1M7 Computer Station in the final release. Even in the more detailed levels, the dark mood of *DOOM* is mostly absent (this is taking on board the part-built nature of the environments, the lack of combat, and the lack of audio, of course).

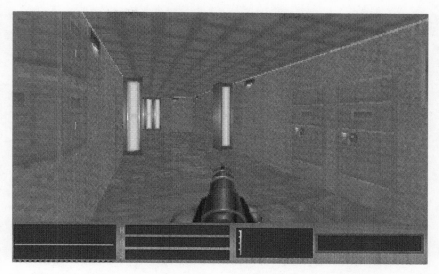

Fig 2. E1M1 from the 0_4 alpha version of *DOOM*, showing light, science-fiction stylings

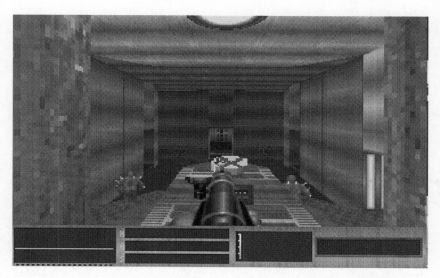

Fig 3. E1M1 from the 0_4 alpha version of *DOOM*, showing an early split-level set piece featuring adjoining sector design

The three core ingredients of *DOOM*'s design—or, certainly, the springboards from which it leapt away from *Wolfenstein 3D*—are already in place in the first alpha: these are variable and dynamic environments, dynamic lighting, and cut-through sectors. According to the notes accompanying the release, moving sectors (raising and lowering platforms) are already designed into the levels but nonoperational. In fact, it's probably fair to say that these core features were still being explored at this point. Level 1 contains an extended set of spiraling, tunnel-like staircases leading out onto a ledge overlooking another room full of Imps, an early variation on the sector joining that was to be such a signature design piece (fig. 3). It ended up in E2M7, although it was really refined to maximize the impact of interior/exterior scales for the opening of E1M1 Hangar.

If the first level is a tantalizing glimpse at what these new techniques might be able to achieve, level 4 is a genuine portal into the future. It's certainly the most assured, polished level in the first alpha and contains the first real moment where split sectors and variable heights create a real wow factor. Turning right from the starting point, the player emerges from a corridor onto a ledge projecting over a lake of nukage (fig. 4). The room is vast and enclosed, with other wings of the complex forming the boundaries of the lake. In the walls of these other structures are windows, not just texture windows, but genuine windows you can see through. Although there aren't any moving dangerous agents to fight at this point, the implications are right there: holes in walls allow line of sight, sound, and, perhaps most important, bullets—in both directions. In *Wolfenstein 3D*, there really wasn't much scope for strategy, apart from the odd instance of perhaps choosing not to enter a room full of machine-gun-toting SS officers with only twenty-three health units and six bullets in the pistol or leading a Hitler ghost away from a pack of others to more safely dispatch him. *DOOM* changed things significantly. Suddenly, the multilevel split sectors enabled a more intelligent approach to be considered. But it didn't slow things down particularly, and it certainly wasn't an indication that the action was going to be less fast paced or desperate. If anything, it ramped up the tension by letting the player know that, sooner or later, they were going to have to hit that room and all it contained. Sure, the odd bit of long-range sniping became possible, but it also meant you could be picked off at a distance by an Imp's fireball. The split sectors meant sound leaked, so it was a pretty safe bet that if you could hear the demons, they could hear you.

Romero describes this "sound flooding" as an entirely new way of activating enemies, a subtly unique feature that maximized the atmosphere (and the artificial intelligence) of the system, creating the impression that, unlike *Wolfenstein 3D*, this wasn't just a hostile, heavily defended environment for players to force their way through but a more balanced, less comfortable situation. While *DOOM* was to be essentially a badass, shotgun-toting demon hunt, it was pretty clear that you were being hunted right back. According to Romero, sound flooding was hardwired into sector design for most levels.

> We used sound zones in *Wolfenstein 3D* as another way to alert enemies to your presence. In *DOOM,* we did the same thing but used sectors as the conduits of audio travel. This was a really important part of making the game scary, as sound could leak all over the place and alert demons. You might see lots of little sector pipes that connect sectors together just to alert monsters—sectors that you'd never see because we put them way up high in the corner of a room. So, we paid a lot of attention to the sound flooding. (JR)

Jump forward a month to the second alpha release, 0_5 (May 22, 1993). This time, we are presented with six levels, even though we've got no monsters moving around (they are in the levels, but just as static sprites). The HUD has changed again. Now we have placeholders for four ammo types (bullets, shells, missiles, and cells) and, over on the right, some intriguingly arcade-like placeholders for time, lives, and score. Of the last three counters, only the one for time made it into the final version of the game, and I will return to the cult of the speedrun in due course. Carmack sees the process of these aspects being removed as indicative of id understanding that they were beginning to move into distinctly new territory.

> In many ways, we were still in the arcade design experience. It's funny if you look back on it—*DOOM* was the first major game that did away with lives. *Wolfenstein 3D* still had lives and 1-ups, and we only realized in there—we're not taking quarters from people, they should be able to keep playing the game, we don't want to send them back to the beginning, we've got save games. . . . *DOOM* is more of exploring the world. Although there are things like getting the 100 percent counts, and the par times [target times for completing each level] still had a reasonably important role in *DOOM*. And it is interesting in recent years to see the resurgence of achievements. (JC)

Fig 4. E1M4 from the 0_4 alpha version of *DOOM*, showing the large enclosed acid lake and windowed structures visible from the player's location

Eventually, scoring would be reduced to a percentage for kills and se-crets, but not just yet. Once the game opens, we have a new function, the automap (created by *DOOM*'s other coder, Dave Taylor). We also have ani-mated and functional acid (causing damage to the player), more dynamic lighting, and working switches. Transition between levels shows us an em-bryonic level map (fig. 5), which would serve as the background for an-nouncing level names, kills, secrets, and timings against par (I'll go into more detail on that later).

Level 2 gives us floor trip switches, secret doors, item pickups, and mov-ing environments. The third part of the design triumvirate is now in place: floors rise and fall, enabling access to split-level environments, drops into new areas, and hidden locations to be suddenly revealed. At this point, many of the levels are recognizable versions of those found in the final re-lease (level 2 is E1M2 Containment Area more or less as is). The move-ment forward is perhaps less marked—it was released only a month later than 0_4, after all—but the design is starting to come together. The use of split levels, dynamic lighting, moving environments, and split sectors can be seen as informing a design style that has now moved fully away from *Wolfenstein 3D* and is as obsessed with the vertical axis as with the horizon-

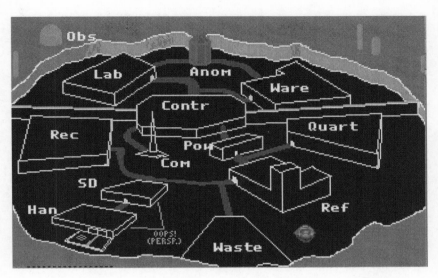

Fig 5. The interlevel map screen from the 0_5 alpha version of DOOM

tal (fig. 6). Gone are the linked series of independent rooms and corridors. Instead, there is a more organic, integrated network of sectors that spill into one another, lie over and around each other, and operate together to create environments with distinct flavors and feels. Whereas *Wolfenstein 3D*'s world was largely interchangeable (a backdrop to the action and little else), *DOOM*'s world had its own identity, a part to play in the experience. Even if the members of the id team were ditching most of the complexities of Hall's original vision in terms of plot and character, they had leapt seismically forward in their understanding of the importance of set design.

Five months pass before the next outing of the game, and it's the final prelaunch press demo, password protected and time-locked to no later than October 31, 1993. It has three levels, one from each episode (E1M2, E2M2, and E3M5), in their more or less finished forms. We still have more Hell-styled artifacts kicking around the joint; we have a different fire mode for the Big Fucking Gun (BFG); we have working monsters, with Zombies, Hell Barons, Lost Souls, and Cacodemons joining the party; and we still have a score counter, displayed in the automap function (with scores ranging from Zombies at 200 points to Hell Barons at 10,000). An items counter also remains in the HUD bar, but apart from that, it's the final version (the items

Fig 6. The 0_5 alpha version of *DOOM,* showing increased complexity in environment design

and score features are entirely separate as well). On finishing each level, a working version of the interlevel map is presented, with scores for kills, items, and secrets. A bonus and score are also featured, as well as time and par time. The level is linked to a feature on the map with the words "You were here."

In terms of features and functions, the pre-beta stands more or less alongside the final game. Not every monster is implemented, lifts and doors move at about half speed, the BFG is more of a souped-up plasma gun than a room-clearing one-shot weapon, and we're still seeing score and item counters being kicked around, but this is essentially *DOOM* as we now know it. Even without audio, the mood is there: dark, fast, tense. The design ethos is all in place: twisting corridors open up into large split-level rooms, and exterior and interior sections allow for radically different senses of scale to exist within a single level. Switches trigger doors at remote locations, making the automap a genuinely useful feature and allowing for the monster closets to make their first appearances. Suddenly, the game is about looking up to find an Imp fireballing you from a high ledge, looking down as a lift drops you into a dark pit you can't shoot into but know is full of Pinkys, feeling your way around in half light until strobing lights suddenly announce the presence of a Cacodemon (although it was that seething wet hiss that really made them the stuff of nightmares), and a well-placed rocket turning a room full of Zombies into a rain of beefy chunklets.

There was one addition to the list of casualties for anyone who had battled and blasted their way through the press demo. In the credits for the game, Sandy Petersen was now on the list as designer, but the creative director wasn't. Tom Hall had gone.

CHAPTER 4

The Fastest Texture Mapping in Town

id Tech 1

The design of *DOOM* was creating level architectures the likes of which no one had ever seen, and these were resting on some groundbreaking technological foundations. The *DOOM* engine, id Tech 1, was responsible for pushing texture and lighting further than any previous PC engine and at a speed that was unheard of outside consoles. The latter was due to the introduction of the humble binary space partition (BSP) to gaming. By introducing BSPs, id ensured that the engine itself would go down in gaming history, regardless of the actual game.

The atomic unit of id Tech 1 is a vertex, a position in a three-dimensional space. Vertexes join to create lines called linedefs. When you add a height variable to a linedef, this (two-dimensional) vertical space running along the linedef is called a sidedef. These are what textures are mapped onto. Once all vertexes are joined by linedefs, you create a polygon, called a sector, each with its own height variable and lighting. Also, just as every sidedef can be texture mapped, so can the "floor" and "ceiling" areas defined by the sector's shape, called visplanes. Finally, you can cut holes in sidedefs to create windows and doors, with the result that light and sound bleed from one sector to another (fig. 7). The engine does not create true three-dimensional maps, in that sectors cannot be placed on top of one another, but it is still remarkably powerful in creating the illusion of vertically stacked environments. *DOOM*'s engine dispensed with the need for absolute right angles and orthogonality between aspects of the environment as found in *Wolfen-*

stein 3D, but it was still locked to absolute vertical and horizontal: there were no sloping floors or ceilings. This meant that runs of texture mapping were applied across fixed planes, and each shift in ceiling or floor height (including dynamically moving objects such as lifts) were, in effect, distinct sectors. John Romero explains,

> The *DOOM* engine—the largest break [was that] all the previous games had been tiled based in the way the levels were created and *DOOM* used a free-form two-dimensional, or it became coined 2.5D, where you could have a 2D layout with different floor and ceiling heights. And it also had textured floors and ceilings and it had the ability to have different light levels in different areas rather than just a uniform light falloff that would start bright and then go dimmer, so we could have the flashing light areas and we could also dynamically move floors and ceilings without an impact on performance. We were still constrained by not being able to move around the two-dimensional line segments, so you couldn't do a swinging door—all the doors had to be things which would just rise up or down. But without impacting the rendering speed at all, we could have free-form changes in any of the lighting levels and any of the heights. And a lot of the things that became the core gameplay elements of *DOOM* were based on changing those things dynamically. (JC)

The freedom to define things like corner angles and ceiling/floor heights already shifted *DOOM* away from *Wolfenstein 3D* dramatically, but two other factors made the environment radically different. Sidedefs were split into three sections: top, middle, and bottom. While a normal wall only needed to utilized the middle section, cut-throughs used all three, creating more opportunity to add detail to the map rather than relying purely on sprites. So it was possible for any given vertical surface to contain three distinct textures. While the more general solution was to simply paint more than one texture onto a single texture sheet rather than add more vertices, the idea that a wall could change texture according to how high up you were was still a conceptual shift. The result is a more broadly detailed environment that made the most of texture mapping. Textures themselves were, of course, something id had been using for a couple of years; John Carmack had wanted to use the idea since 1990. Following *Hovertank 3D,* which lacked any kind of textures, he was looking to push forward to the next problem. As Romero puts it,

Fig 7. A vertex (1), linedef (2), sidedef (3), and part of a visplane (4) in
DOOM's E1M1

And so that's why *Catacomb 3D* was texture mapped, because of this
"what are you going to do next"; it needed to get a plus-plus. That was
EGA texture mapping, which is actually much harder than VGA texture
mapping. So the first texture-mapped FPS game out was actually *Catacomb 3D*, not *Ultima*. *Ultima Underworld* came out at the end of April
'92, and one week later we came out with *Wolfenstein 3D*, with our VGA
texture mapping. They did the first VGA texture mapping, but we did
the first [EGA] texture mapping with *Catacomb 3D* in '91. (JR)

The fact that this kind of competition over graphics standards persists
twenty years later gives some indication of the importance of texture mapping to games. More to the point, Romero's comments reinforce the idea
that *Catacomb 3D* was a stepping-stone, a chance to push the technology
forward rather than a focused, designed game experience. The real fruition
came with *Wolfenstein 3D*. And, to be fair, we do need to give credit to Blue
Sky's game: after all, it did have texture mapping on the floors and ceilings
as well as the walls, and it did have angled floors and variable heights; and
although it's not the roller coaster that *DOOM* is, it's not actually *that* slow.
This is an interesting point, however, as the fact that *Ultima Underworld*

isn't necessarily sluggish by contemporary standards may say more about a general drop in speed in FPS games since *DOOM,* or at least in a significant number of them—something we might attribute to *Halo* and the rise of the console shooter. For Carmack, the issue is not one of innovation per se but of applied engineering.

> No one in gaming invented texture mapping. You can say that earlier games like *Wing Commander* [Origin 1990], had scaled-sprite graphics and scaling a bit-map is texture mapping of a sort, it's just limited. The more unique bit in the *Wolfenstein 3D* and *DOOM* approaches was that they made the sacrifice of the degrees of freedom to get a higher performance. . . . The design choice I made with all of our early games up till *Quake* was that the important ability is moving you around in the world, and you really don't need as much the ability to roll your head or have these sloping geometries, and if you make that restriction, there's very significant improvement you can make. Engineering is about trade-offs, we can sacrifice this to get this, and smart engineering is when you recognize that you get more than you're trading for; you're getting good value. (JC)

Anyway, *DOOM*'s texture mapping was a case of complexity and vision feeding into one another. The color palette for the game is initially very muted—*Wolfenstein 3D* is positively garish in comparison (fig. 8)—with grays, browns, and metals dominating (fig. 9). This was hardwired into the engine build, a clear-cut case of the fusion of artistic and technical development going hand in hand. The idea, according to Carmack was to lock the palette down to a smaller selection, to give the trade-off of being able to ensure that you could retain quality, as lighting "would smoothly ramp down through the lighting [falloff]."

In terms of the actual textures being mapped into the game, there was a subtle revolution occurring. Adrian Carmack and Kevin Cloud were using the new graphical capabilities available to them to explore new concepts in designing and selecting textures. This exploration centered around the use of photographic and scanned material to form the basis of the textures, an idea that flows naturally from the attempt to model "real-world" spaces that was an early focus of the DOOM Bible. Cloud explains,

> A lot of games had very vibrant colour palettes, a very cartoon concept.

Fig 8. *Wolfenstein 3D*'s high-contrast texturing

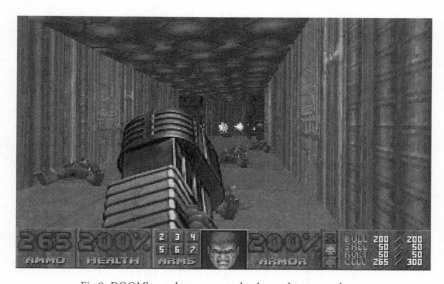

Fig 9. *DOOM*'s much more muted color and texture scheme

And the thing that was hitting us at the time was all this new scanning, at least from my perspective, which was giving a really gritty, realistic look to the art. We had all these limited colors and all these games that are looking the same, and we wanted to see could we break out of that and really create something a bit more gritty and dirty. So a lot of our things began with a source of scanned material. We'd find lots of pieces of things to scan in even just to set up a color palette or to give us a background texture. That really wasn't happening back then very much—there wasn't a lot of use of photo reference in games—and it really gave us a different style direction that was a little more gritty than what people were used to. (KC)

That's not to say that *DOOM* wasn't fairly abstract or vivid in places. Sandy Petersen brought a whole new feel to proceedings by adding bright clashes of primary color as he introduced more hellish architecture to the world (in the alphas, Hell's influence was largely represented by sprites—items scattered around the world as well as the monsters invading it). As the episodes progress, colors get more and more intense and primary, and the architecture becomes less science fiction and more gothic. It's also probably the only game out there to feature a close-up photograph of a game developer's elbow as a skin wall (the elbow in question belongs to Cloud, who says, "That's just the way we rolled back then").

The fact that, unlike *Wolfenstein 3D*, id Tech 1 was now using visplanes to map textures across the floors and ceilings certainly contributes a great deal to the flavor of the game, assisting with a sense of cramped claustrophobia to the corridor crawls and then contrasting this with "real-world photo" textures mapped onto giant backdrop sidedefs—the precursor to skyboxes (two-dimensional backdrop images wrapped around the level to create a sense of scale, basically analogous to mattes in cinema).[1] The shift between interior and exterior spaces drives the sense of scale in the game, reinforcing the more subtle and constant variations in ceiling and floor heights. Attaching damage to visplanes was another new feature that, coupled with simple animated textures, gave the world nukage and lava alongside crushing ceilings and walls. This may seem simple in retrospect, but it represents a huge leap forward in terms of the spaces that were being represented. Even without agents, the environment could present more of a challenge than just navigating around it. *DOOM* might have been all about the arcades, but inadvertently or not, it created the basic technological and design tools that were to initiate the deviation of FPS games away from this basic form into games like first-person survival horror such as *Amnesia: The Dark Descent* (Frictional Games 2010), physics puzzlers like *Portal*, and platformers like *Mirror's Edge*.[2]

The other major new factor in controlling both gameplay and atmosphere that marked the new engine apart was lighting. id Tech 1 allowed for two distinct lighting designs that gave gameplay a unique feeling .The first was variable levels. Whereas *Wolfenstein 3D* took place under flat, bright strip lights and whereas *Ultima Underworld* was a uniform smudge of dim illumination, *DOOM*'s environments contrasted not just in scale but in darkness. An automatic drop-off into darkness helped enhance the illusion of vertical space and horizontal distance. Particularly when used in combination with sound flooding, darkness assisted in the sense that the levels were large, holistic environments (rather than a series of set pieces). As a design tool, it created distinction and enabled foreshadowing to be used to powerfully sculpt the player's experience. There was little more terrifying than the sound of monsters growling somewhere in the dark or the prospect of entering a dark room from a light one. Although *DOOM* didn't have any kind of stealth system, contrast between dark and well-lit areas and co-opting these for tactical advantage in combat were to become staples of the genre in years to come. This culminates in Looking Glass Studios' *Thief* games (1998, 2000), where the *s* of FPS stands for "stealth," not "shooter." Attaching light levels independently to each sector allowed for far greater control over how similarly textured areas might be represented. Coupled with the lighting drop-off, this created a sense of pervasive gloom throughout the environments, which, for Romero, was fundamental to the feel of the levels.

> Out of all the engines I've seen, it's almost the perfect engine for creating levels that are almost forced into being in-theme with the game. Because the engine itself has diminished lighting along the distance, so you can set the lighting for different sectors but the game is going to darken them as the distance goes out, on purpose, . . . the game is going to render them scary whether you like it or not. So that was a very different thing that most people had never seen: a diminished lighting engine model. (JR)

If diminishing lighting forced a scary edge to the levels, then strobing and flickering lights, not to mention the combination of abrupt lighting shifts with environmental triggers, allowed the level design to tip over into panic-inducing. As a second feature of the enhanced lighting in the engine, being able to turn lights on and off in real time once again added considerable scope to the designer's toolkit. The challenge was balancing these new features, all of which had the potential for slowing down play. Each added new things for the player to have to consider, least of all whether it was such a good idea to enter into an area that was periodically plunged into epilepsy-inducing bursts of strobing darkness; and the results would automatically change, to some extent, *Wolfenstein 3D*'s run-and-gun flavor. What is important about both the new ways of creating variable environments (including moving sectors to create lifts, raising floors, and crushing ceilings, as well as steps and drops) and the new ways of manipulating light is that the technology pushed forward the opportunity for design. A new type of game environment was made possible, and in many ways, Romero and Petersen's exploration of these new potentials drove the design of *DOOM*. It's a classic example of the interplay between technological advance and creative practice, which defines the games industry perhaps more than any other medium.

Together, vertexes, linedefs, sidedefs, sectors, and their associated variables broadly define the level, but the situation becomes more complicated when it comes to the actual business of representing everything in real time, and this is where the real genius of John Carmack's engine comes through. A game's fps (frames per second) rate refers to the number of times everything visible on the screen is redrawn. A faster fps rate basically means faster, more responsive action, less jerky animation, and a smoother, quicker experience. This was the unholy grail for DOOM. Any game's engine has to work out what is being presented to the player x number of times per second, factoring in any changes in location or representation of its elements. That's on top of all the background, unrepresented data, integers, and algorithms going on—we're just talking graphics. A WAD file (a level file for *DOOM*—the acronym stands for "Where's All the Data") is basically a set of instructions that tell the game how to display the level— literally, "draw a point here, and here; join them together and attach texture a to a height of b pixels; then join all of these together and cover the floor in this sector with texture c, the ceiling with texture d, and apply lighting e," and so on. This is redrawn x number of times per second. Obviously, this is a fairly complex process, and then designers add in a player moving around, agents moving around, fireballs flying about, barrels exploding, lifts rising and falling, and so on. One of the methods of cutting down on the computation per second is to only render what is visible to a player, which simply reduces the quantity of data that requires processing. But this still leaves a substantial amount of work to happen, and this is where frame rates can drop, creating a visual lag that basically demolishes the experience of play. According to Romero, it was this that "revealed a limitation in the way Carmack was rendering the scene, because he was using lists of sectors for drawing, and I drew something that had recursive sectors and that made the game go really slow" (JR).

The list Romero refers to is one where every sector in the WAD is given a unique identifier so that the rendering engine can look up exactly what it is supposed to render and how. The problem is that if an engine is rendering every sector, it is doing unnecessary work. Equally, if it renders every object within a field of view, the normal way of doing this (called the painter's algorithm) is to start with drawing the background, then draw the set of objects next farthest from the player, and so on right up to the foreground. Another way of thinking about this is to imagine it like a set of Photoshop layers or sheets of transparent plastic laid in a stack. The secondary issue is, then, that some objects rendered by this process may not actually be visible, if they are behind other objects. In real terms, if a low wall obscures a lava pit but the animated lava texture is being re-rendered forty times a second, that's a lot of completely wasted processing going on, which will slow down the process of rendering the whole scene, compromising the frame rate. Looking for a solution to this during his work on the Super Nintendo port of *Wolfenstein 3D*, Carmack decided to try implementing binary space partitions.

A BSP is basically a way of identifying sectors' relationships to one another to avoid redundant rendering. It shifts the workload needed in calculating which objects are visible from given perspectives in the level to the end of the editing process, which culminates in the creation of a BSP table that contains the data the rendering engine requires to establish the correct sequence and need for object rendering, thus avoiding this having to be carried out in real time, as the game runs. The BSP breaks the level right down into units called subsectors, which are polygons contained within each sector. Each subsector has a list of sectors associated with it. The rendering engine moves down the tree until it finds a subsector, then checks against associated sectors, rather than having to work out associations in "longhand," so to speak, each time it redraws the screen. In essence, a BSP functions a little like an index in a book, allowing associations, dependencies, and hierarchies to be quickly and easily found. As such, like any kind of indexing algorithm, BSPs are phenomenally powerful in reducing rendering time and, therefore, upping the frame rate. Traditionally, Carmack's "discovery" of BSPs is attributed to the work of Bruce Naylor, who had published a number of papers on BSPs in the early 1980s, although he references a manual, conceptual model for BSPs, or an "incipient version" (Naylor 1981) suggested by Schumacker over a decade earlier (Schumacker 1969, 142). Carmack, however, says he first came across the idea in *Computer Graphics: Principles and Practice* (Foley et al. 1990) and had been puzzling over it for some time. His experience of implementing BSPs is worth recounting, as it paints a vivid picture of the pre-World Wide Web computer science scene of the time.

> It's not a really supercritical aspect of it, but it is interesting that when I did the early work on BSPs, Bruce Naylor came down and visited here and gave me copies of a bunch of his papers. It's interesting to talk to people about the old days. Of course, you've got the Internet now. You can find anything nowadays. But back then, it was really something to get reprints of old academic papers. There were some clearinghouses I used to use: you'd pay twenty-five dollars or whatever, and they'd mail you xeroxes of old research papers. It was just a very, very different world. I learned most of my programming when I had a grand total of like three reference books. You had to figure everything else yourself. So I was finding I was reinventing a lot of classic things, like Huffman encoding or LZW encoding. So I'd be all proud of myself for having figured something out, and then I'd find it was just classic method and they did it better than I did. (JC)

Integrating BSPs meant Carmack had co-opted the technology for gaming for the very first time, and the impact of this solution has been hardwired into the core of a huge number of game engines since then. Along with *DOOM*'s many other contributions, Carmack's adoption of the binary space partition to games is an extraordinary legacy for the medium. What were the results? As Romero puts it simply, "That's when everything went superfast and the BSP was born for computer games." In his typical fashion, Carmack is far less willing than others to see his contribution in quite such a groundbreaking light.

> People like to look for the magic special sauce. They like to look for that narrative. But for almost anything, there are multiple valid ways to get to the same end result. And *DOOM* started off with a different approach that wasn't getting the speed I wanted. I first used BSPs on the Super

Nintendo *Wolfenstein 3D* port, where I had to come up with more speed than the raycasting approach. And then when I came back to working on *DOOM*, I wound up working in that way because it seemed like a good approach. Conversely though, the Build engine (*Duke Nukem 3D*) didn't use BSPs, and it was every bit as effective as the way *DOOM* was implemented. But certainly because of *DOOM*'s success, thousands of people learned what BSP trees were and followed up on some of those academic threads. (JC)

As a final point, it's worth bearing in mind how long many of the techniques that came to fruition in *DOOM* had been gathering pace in the background. Carmack himself sees a relatively smooth curve from the earliest work on *Hovertank 3D* in terms of achieving a vision of where 3D gaming could go. Cloud reaffirms this:

John, I think, knew. John has an uncanny ability to be able to see things that are happening in computers and games and be able to predict ahead. I think you have to have that talent to be a successful engineer, 'cause you are working on things that may not see the light of day for four, five, six years. And some of the things he's doing today he talked about ten years ago. (KC)

Whether you accept Carmack's line that someone else would have done it if he hadn't or the more traditional "special sauce narrative," it is clear that game technology and game design fused in a particularly magical and effective way in idTech1. The result is history.

CHAPTER 5

DOOM by Numbers

DOOM is a game of wonderful simplicity in many dimensions, not just story and gameplay. The entire first episode, Knee Deep in the Dead, contains just six monsters, one of which only appears in the very final level, in a kind of boss battle. All of *DOOM*'s monsters are defined by a number of parameters, although the artificial intelligence is, by modern terms, very simple.[1] Defining parameters include height and width (to establish bounding boxes so they act as obstacles), speed, reaction time, pain delay on being hit, a series of links to audiovisual files for audio and animation, and, of course, hit points and damage.

All damage is randomly calculated within a given spread, as is the likelihood of the monster hitting its target (which is adjusted by range to target). For example, the Trooper has 20 hit points, causes 3–15 damage per successful shot, moves at 70 map units per second (MUS), and so on. The Imp, in comparison, is considerably tougher. He has 60 hit points, moves at 93 MUS, and has two attacks: a melee, causing 3–24 damage, and a slow-moving projectile, whose speed is calculated at 350 MUS and also causes 3–24 damage. It should be noted that unlike the Trooper's bullets, the Imp's fireball attack is slow enough to be dodged. The artificial intelligence exhibits basic pathfinding and target acquisition, but there is no tactical behavior as we understand it in more contemporary games. Players had to wait until *Half-Life* for the uneasy realization that they had just been flanked. Interesting, though, is how simple tricks helped bootstrap the sense of intelligence of the agents upward. For example, *DOOM*'s monsters will happily attack one another. If a Trooper happens to be in the line of fire between an Imp and the player, the Trooper will get hit by the Imp's fireball, and provided this doesn't prove fatal, the Trooper is likely to forget all about the player and attack back. This is really very basic in AI terms, but it creates a sense of interrelationship that is comparatively powerful, and it perfectly fitted the frenzied chaos that Romero wanted to create.

> That was never seen in a game before, . . . that they are so possessed, they are so out of their minds that they kill each other. They don't care what they kill, they just want to kill everything, even each other. (JR)

As an aside, the process of monster creation fell mostly to Adrian Carmack, with Kevin Cloud focusing mainly on weapons (textures and details were shared). Concept sketches were passed onto Gregor Puntchaz, who turned them into latex models that were manipulated to create the basis for sprite animation. As we've seen, many of the basic sprites and animations existed very early on in development, and according to Cloud, there was never a particularly formal process of creation, test, and iteration.

> Sandy and John [Romero] would have an idea of something that they wanted in the game, like a cool weapon or a character, there'd be some brief discussions, and then we'd just turn each other loose and do something about it. It wasn't as if ideas couldn't come from everywhere, but generally they came from Sandy and John and then Adrian and I focused on the art. But for the most part, even though there was some pretty different style and skill differences, people pretty much let each other do their thing. Sandy and John weren't like "We want it to look like this," more "We want a shotgun," so we'd go off and make a shotgun and just get it into the game. There's wasn't a lot of reworking. It was more like "Hey, I've got this cool idea, let's put it in the game." (KC)

The idea of a small team running around more or less freely is like a utopian dream, and we do need to remember the context the members of the id team were operating in (and, arguably, the old adage that very talented people have a sickening ability to make stuff look really easy). But once again, we can see the links to the current indie boom, as the experimental approach is very appealing, in terms of a group of like-minded experts experimenting sometimes wildly with each others' output. Cloud also tellingly notes that at this point in the history of game development, the lack of a drive toward transferable intellectual property and the requirement of extendable franchises was liberating and also served to simply make a better game.

> We would create the textures, and sometimes a wall would end up on the floor and a floor would end up on the ceiling. . . . I mean, the environments were such an abstraction. It was just crazy. There were candelabras on a space station. It made no sense. The design direction kind of ebbed and moved and changed over time, and we riffed on new ideas as we were moving along. . . . You went with the flow of it. It was a great way of working at that point, because there was really no expectation of anything, and games weren't—well, no one was trying to make a movie. And it allowed you to focus on what works, not what doesn't work, which is a nice frame of mind to be in—OK, that works, let's do more of that, not "That doesn't work and we've GOT to have that in, so let's fix it." We'd be more like "That doesn't work, so screw it. We won't do that. We'll do more of this." (KC)

On the flip side of things, the player has access to a range of weapons and objects as well as their 100 hit points and good ol' fists. Armor is expressed as a percentage, with green armor absorbing one-third of all damage taken. The blue mega-armor raises the percentage to 200 percent and absorbs half of the damage. Armor bonuses raise the current armor's percentage by 1 percent, up to a maximum of 200 percent. Health vials (+1 percent), stimpacks (+10 percent), and medikits (+25 percent) allow the player to regain lost health. There are a range of super power-ups. Some of these give temporary benefits: partial invisibility, invincibility, radiation suits to prevent damage from nukage, light amplification goggles. Others, like the soul sphere or automap, give a one-off boost, and the backpack permanently increases ammo capacity. Then there are, of course, the guns.

DOOM's weapons break down into two types: hitscans and projectiles. The latter have a speed, meaning they can be avoided by a fast player, but also meaning monsters' speeds and positions must be accounted for when they are being used. A hitscan is calculated at the moment of firing and cannot be avoided. Of the weapons in Episode 1, the fist, chainsaw, pistol, shotgun, and chaingun are all hitscans. The fist and chainsaw are both unlimited melee weapons with a range of 64 units that do 2–20 damage per hit. The chainsaw increases the number of hits per minute from roughly 123 to 525, so it's similar to the chaingun, which uses the same ammo and does the same damage as the pistol (5–15 units) but increases the fire rate from 150 shots per minute to 525. Unlike melee weapons, hitscan distance weapons include shot dispersal when the fire key is held down, so subsequent shots have a greater chance of going wide (introducing a sense of recoil). The shotgun is slightly different, as it includes a spreading set of seven bullets (each sticking to the 5–15 hitscan damage of the pistol). This means that depending on range to the target, multiple enemies can be hit with a single shot. At close range, the majority of the bullets will hit the same target, increasing the damage toward a massive potential of 105. Balancing this, however, is a much slower rate of fire—around 57 shots per minute. Finally, Episode 1 also includes a single projectile weapon, the rocket launcher. Its rockets are twice the speed of an Imp's and include a splash damage feature. Each rocket causes 20–160 damage on impact but also triggers an area blast, which starts at 128 damage at the epicenter and decreases outward to 128 units (so a monster standing 100 units away would take 28 damage). Balancing against this massive damage to a directly hit target is the fact that the player can also be caught in the blast, and there is a slow rate of fire (105 shots per minute). While explaining all this weapon detail here might seem like nerding out somewhat, it's actually really important to consider how *DOOM* manages its arsenal of weapons, items, and monsters, because it's this subtle balance, not just a great concept and good design, that makes a game really work. The process of getting this balance right occupied the *DOOM* team for some time, and for Cloud, it's inherently tied to how immersive *DOOM* is. A comment of his really brings home how complex reactions can emerge from the carefully managed interplay of integers:

> A lot of time was spent thinking about the weapons and how they played off against the creatures, the weapon switch speeds, the weapon damage, enemy placement, in terms of trying to get those types of emotional reactions that are not just cognitive but emotional. (KC)

Equally, managing the sense of development across a game's duration is critical, and getting either the pacing of new features or the balance between increasing difficulty and increasing player capabilities wrong can seriously unbalance a game, destroying any sense of atmosphere, challenge, or fun. For example, *Prey* (Humanhead Studios 2006) really suffered from this, although it's hard to exactly put your finger on why. On paper, *Prey* does things right, it adds new weapons just before it introduces new aliens, so you get the rush of power as a reward before the difficulty ramps up, it keeps back old friends even while adding new foes, and the weapons have a qualitatively different feel and flavor and clear tactical uses in various situations. But it just doesn't quite hang together, and in the face of an almost total lack of serious academic analysis of the minutiae of mechanic balancing, we'll have to settle with the folk understanding and intuiting that most designers and players have about getting the balance right and how important it is.

One of the things *DOOM* does that has not, interestingly, become a standardized FPS design tactic is "leaking" weapons forward in secret areas, essentially rewarding players for exploration at the risk of throwing off game balance. Especially given what I've just argued, the idea of allowing a rocket launcher to be discovered by players in E1M3, some four levels before other players are certain to find it in E1M7, is a high-risk strategy and arguably demonstrates how effective the game is at balance on a general level.[2] Certainly, more modern games that have a set number of weapons and use these as a reward system, such as *Quake 4* (Raven Software 2004) or *Half-Life 2,* are designed to make sure that when the player obtains the weapon is carefully orchestrated, even if they subsequently allow a degree of tactical choice in terms of how combat is approached. *DOOM* doesn't bother with any of that. The rocket launcher appears as a secret in E1M3–6 and is officially found in E1M7; the shotgun is a secret in E1M1 and official in the subsequent level; the chaingun is a secret in E1M2–3 and official in E1M4; and the chainsaw is a secret in E1M2, 3, and 5 and official in E1M6. So for nonexploring players, there is a staggering of new weapons—shotgun on 2, chaingun on 4, chainsaw on 6, and rocket launcher on 7—but the rewards of exploration deliver these much, much earlier. Equally, the limited number of monsters in Episode 1 are staggered on lower difficulty settings, but this changes as one hits the Ultra Violence or Nightmare levels. Shotgun Troopers or Sergeants normally appear in E1M3, but in the higher settings, they are right there from the outset. Demons, or Pinkys (as they are more commonly known), pop up in E1M3, but their invisible counterparts, Spectres, appear in E1M6 for lowest difficulty, E1M5 for midrange, and E1M3 for supertough. The final monster in Episode 1, the Baron of Hell, appears as a boss for all difficulty settings in E1M8. For the sake of consistency, we should note that Pinkys have 150 hit points and are fast movers (at 175 MUS), with a single melee attack dealing 4–40 damage (Spectres are exactly the same). Sergeants come in slightly tougher than standard Troopers, with 30 hit points and a shotgun attack similar to the player's, dealing 3–15 damage per bullet, with a potential total of 9–45. Barons have a whopping 1,000 hit points, move at the same speed as an Imp, and also have both melee and missile attacks. The former deals 10–80 damage; the latter is a projectile with a speed of 525 MUS, doing 8–64 damage on impact.

Remember all that now, as we descend into Hell. There will be tests later. Seriously though, it is important to bear these kinds of details in mind, as they do inform design considerably. From the geographic placement of monsters within a level to the dynamics of multiple and especially mixed multiple monster groups, not to mention the golden threads pulling players around the game space, the details may exist under the hood, but their influence on game design and gameplay is total. In games, the integer is king.

CHAPTER 6

A Soundtrack for Mayhem

Bobby Prince, *DOOM*'s composer and audio wizard, had been working with id since the *Keen* days, picking up the job via Scott Miller. This early work was notable for two things. First, it was conducted largely in the dark. Prince told me, "We did a lot of our contact by long distance . . . by them sending me print outs of their early artwork. For *Keen,* I never saw the game until it was completed."[1] Second (and perhaps more remarkable) is the way in which early game sound was created. At this point, the process of composition was as much about tool development as it was any notion of traditional music creation.

Working with early general MIDI, Prince and his contemporaries had to create the software to run their work and had to create work that fitted the capabilities of the software as they went along. He notes that for the second *Keen* game, the audio was created using iMuse, a program Romero wrote for the purpose, creating a waveform from data and routing it through the computer's speakers (Romero says, "It let us designers basically draw the sound on the screen with the mouse. We could immediately play it back, tweak it, and save it when it sounded right"). The results were certainly minimalist, a real triumph of ingenuity in the face of extreme technological constraints. Games shipped with a 360-kilobyte ceiling in terms of file size. This meant that any audio had to be stripped back to the absolute minimum, making every note count. Creating an eight-bar loop that doesn't drive the player insane after a few minutes of repetition is a compositional challenge. Prince estimates that every note cost around 5 bytes, so

I literally had to go in and sometimes take a note out of a chord, or very selectively pick a note that wasn't really that important or might have been blocked by another note or sound, and just hand tweak it so I could get it down to a size that would fit along with the game itself. (BP)

To put this another way, imagine composing a piece for an orchestra that charges by the note, on a shoestring budget, with the added requirement that you have to build the instruments as you go along. id and Prince did receive some help from manufacturers of sound cards, who were eager to see products that showed off their new technology to its very best, but it was still a very limited affair that frequently comes across as architectural design as much as composition.[2] Finding appropriate gaps in the tonal range of the sound was a crucial aspect of the work, to ensure that the limited audio available didn't blur into a muddy noise. The results were often frustrating; Prince likens the snare effects of the Nazi theme song in *Wolfenstein 3D* to a "little windup bear." Yet he suggests that the challenge was often equally inspiring.

But another interesting aspect of it . . . is when you are limited, often it's easier to come up with something than when you have anything available. You can get lost in a huge or infinite palette. When you're locked in a little bit, and somehow, with the early games (*Wolfenstein 3D* wasn't for kids but *Keen* definitely was), the sounds really sounded right for that time and the feel they gave to the game. I don't know that having real instruments play those compositions would ever sound good. Or would sound right, put it that way. (BP)

Perhaps because of all of these challenges or because id knew and trusted his work, Prince was given a very open brief for *DOOM*. Supplied initially with Hall's Bible (later supplemented by examples of Adrian Carmack's artwork), Prince was instructed to create as much music as he could within the timeframe of the brief, along with all the sound and audio effects for the game. We'll deal with the music first.

Famously, the members of the id team were huge metal fans, and this greatly influenced the musical backdrop to *DOOM*. Prince notes that Tom Hall leaned slightly more toward classical, and Romero has commented that John Carmack, when it was his turn to control the office stereo, was more into Prince (as in "the artist formerly known as," not Bobby),[3] but essentially *DOOM* was metal through and through. Prince had reservations about this, pushing more for an ambient, environmentally sensitive soundtrack. But he duly supplied a large body of music, including plenty of metalesque scores. Mainly, he says, this was to prove that metal didn't work as well as the darker, moodier pieces. It all went in anyway. Placement of the music fell to Romero, with the result that a significant number of the tracks in *DOOM* were never really intended for the final product and were basically placeholders. Speaking with Prince about this really confirmed for me what I suspected after a few months listening to the soundtrack: that there's a real quality range across the soundtrack. That's not to denigrate any particular track, but it's interesting that some tracks are much more clearly invested in and complete, in terms of layers and diversity of sounds and compositional complexity, and I don't think it's an accident that these tend to be the slower, darker, more ambient pieces that Prince favored. I'm thinking specifically of tracks such as "The Demons from Adrian's Pen" (used in E2M2) or "Nobody Told Me about id" (E2M8). Prince says the track that he feels works best in the game is "Suspense," used in E1M5 Phobos Lab (and later in E4M4 for *Ultimate DOOM*). I'm also rather fond of "Sweet Little Dead Bunny," if only because it sounds like Mr. Bungle, which can only ever be a good thing. It is interesting how, if anything, the technological limitations of the era also helped push the soundtrack away from simply a selection of soundalike metal. Prince recalls,

> There were also limited [instruments]—the guitar sounds were extremely limited. There was basically one overdriven guitar sound in the general MIDI specifications, and there's not much you can do with it. It's very weak and doesn't sound very good, and it gets old to your ear. . . . So I was facing all of those things, and that's the reason it turned out the way it turned out. If it had been digital audio, it would have been totally different. It would have sounded more like a band really did it. (BP)

In many ways, this played into Prince's hands, as he got an opportunity to use more classically influenced structures and sounds, demonstrating that an orchestral sound could be as evil as anything metal could produce. Really, though, underpinning Prince's compositional choices was not any particular musical style but a deep awareness of the functional constraints facing game music. He admits to being the first to turn music off when gaming and argues that the critically important factor was managing the balance of having music that was serving a purpose without being repetitive and obtrusive. As much as anything else, this is a structural issue, like managing how a loop feeds back into itself without drawing attention to the fact that it's looping.

On the flip side of things, whereas the establishment of the metal soundtrack template for first-person shooters had as much to do with Romero and the rest of id, Prince takes full responsibility for setting another template: the unholy concoction of roars, hisses, grunts, and blasts that, nostalgia aside, still make *DOOM*'s audio a standout work. There are two things to say about this really. The first, remarkable thing is that the audio for *DOOM*'s monsters was created more or less in the dark, growing from single-sentence descriptions of the hellish critters supplemented, as work progressed, with sketches from Adrian Carmack and Kevin Cloud. Prince's method was simple, he says; he just imagined what noise each creature would make, "so if you close your eyes, you could see it." But that's just the man being self-deprecating, as the real success of *DOOM*'s sound effects comes from a brilliant understanding of orchestrating sound in a nonlinear space, and perhaps here, the limitations of the space (in terms of file size) in which Prince was operating actually helped things. The total number of sound entities in *DOOM* is tiny, but in a complex level, there can be a fair number of things happening at once, and Prince was careful to try and ensure that different cues were spread across the tonal range, meaning that some would bleed through the music and other audio even at a distance. *DOOM*'s famous doors, which have become so iconic the sound even appeared in a recent Doctor Who episode,[4] are audible even from the far side of some levels, as is the sound of an Imp activating on hearing the player. Although *DOOM*'s audio complexity is clearly not on the scale of a modern game, Prince notes that neither were the programs available to support and manage it, and many of the decisions about balancing audio and not letting important sound cues get buried had to be planned and implemented manually. Interestingly, he remembers that during *DOOM*'s production, John Carmack approached him to suggest that in the next game, music would be absent altogether, with only ambient, environmental noise used to sculpt the player experience. This once again shows how far ahead of the curve id's thinking was, even if the black hole of heavy rock and the temptation of having Trent Reznor write your soundtracks proved a little too attractive in reality.

So let's put all this into context. On one hand, we have *DOOM*'s metal score creating one of the first truly iconic soundtracks in modern gaming. On the other, we have the move toward more ambient, moody, environmentally driven music in games, a long way from the arcade-style soundtracks of earlier efforts. *Doom* still stands as a master class in economic, do-it-yourself sound design. The audio effects were a quantum leap from those of *Wolfenstein 3D* and, for me, are critical to *DOOM*'s sense of world and sense of weight. The latter is one of the toughest design challenges in any virtual or simulated space, one that ranges from simple visual design to animation, artificial intelligence, and physics. Sound can play a huge role in creating a sense of weight, and *DOOM*'s crunching guns and bass bellows certainly do just this, often coming up under the melodic range of the music that is quite flimsy in comparison. Moreover, the audio sews the visuals to a sense of world, which was groundbreaking in intensity. It's hard to quantify exactly what makes the sounds of the Imps and the Cacodemons so well designed, but it's not simply a gameplay association; it's the art of an expert. Alongside the balancing and, particularly, Prince's attention to sound bleeds and overshadows, the artistic decisions sitting behind the final sound of *DOOM*'s audio play a massive part in the sense of immersiveness of the final product. Romero recognizes that *DOOM*'s sound was a "very important" part of the overall experience for the player. For me, in terms of its legacy for gaming, *DOOM* is one of the very first games where audio came out of the background and stood alongside the visuals, creating a world that is as much a product of the audio as of anything else. As Prince puts it, "I really wanted to scare the living hell out of people with the sound alone." When the player steps out of the antechamber in E2M8 and first hears the pounding, slamming, giant-piston steps of the Cyberdemon before they even see the thing, that job is already done.

CHAPTER 7

All Hell Breaks Loose

Launch, Sales, and Critical Reception

We're nearly ready to take a stroll through Hell and hit the game in detail, but before we do that, we need to look at what happened on December 10, 1993, the day that (to hijack W. B. Yeats) a "rough beast, its hour come round at last," slouched onto the University of Wisconsin's FTP system to be born. I've already spent a little time setting the context for *DOOM*'s launch, but it's worth reiterating some of that, for reasons that will become clear.

In 1993, we've got a few home consoles on the market, and they are doing fairly well. Sony is twelve months away from launching the first PlayStation in Japan and twenty-one months from a European and North American release. There is little crossover between console and PC gaming. As Romero noted, PC games are largely more complex, sluggish affairs. Home computer games have, of course, been around since the early 1980s, but graphics as we know them now are still in their comparative infancy. Equally, this is prior to game retail chains and any kind of formal online distribution like Steam. Internet access happens for most users through modems (56.6 kilobytes per second is a reasonable speed), and there's no World Wide Web yet. E-mail is around, of course, as well as text-based things like Gopher, Telnet, bulletin board systems, and the occasional MUD. But there's a hardcore community (or network of communities) online who are already trading information and, more important, files, an embryonic online distribution network. Frans Mäyrä sees this as a time of rapid expansion, arguing that *DOOM*'s success is closely tied to the explosion of the Internet around this time.

There was an increasing demand for content designed for PCs, and these computers were rapidly becoming interconnected into a global communications network. The release of the free *DOOM* shareware version through the Internet and BBS systems benefited from both trends of development. (Mäyrä 2008, 103)

Technically, *DOOM* wasn't shareware, which might sound like splitting hairs, but the technicality is actually pretty important and pays tribute to Scott Miller at Apogee Software, who, in many ways, built the launch ramp *DOOM* took full advantage of. Jim Knopf and Andrew Fluegelman take credit for inventing the shareware scene of the late 1980s and '90s, each independently coming up with the idea to ask users for voluntary donations in return for free distribution and use of their programs. They were swiftly introduced to one another following the public release of their work, coordinated application names (PC-File and PC-Talk), and set a standard suggested donation of twenty-five dollars. The model took off, according to Knopf (1995–96), at a staggering rate. He argues that several factors were responsible: not landing the user with "clumsy copy protection schemes"; lower pricing than commercial retail applications; an extended trial period by the very nature of the system; and independence from retail, giving the model a sense of novelty. At this stage, the term being used for the model was either *freeware* (copyrighted by Fluegelman, so not in general use) or *user-supported software*. In 1984, a competition was launched by Nelson Ford to find an alternative, and *shareware*, reappropriated by Bob Wallace from earlier, pre-IBM usage, came up tops (Ford 2000). Ford was also responsible for the creation of the Association of Shareware Professionals (ASP), formed in 1987, to protect both creators and consumers from less reputable shareware practices. The concept of shareware was simple: you got it for free and then donated to the creator if you liked it. Ironically, although shareware gaming died out in the late '90s, it's seen something of a revival in the last couple of years in the independent game sector, with indie developers asking for donations for their work and occasionally living quite comfortably off the results. The Humble Indie Bundle is a recent case in point.[1]

Right on top of the formation of ASP, shareware was picked up, pioneered, and then adapted into a more robust business model, by Scott Miller and his company Apogee. Miller cut his teeth as a game programmer, with a couple of text-based adventures under his belt, and in 1987, he tried out the new version of sharewaring for the ASCII-graphic top-down action-adventure title *Kingdom of Kroz*. Rather than giving players access to the full game and then retrospectively asking for a donation, Miller released the first episode of the game for free and then charged players to get the rest of it. We can get an idea of how this worked from the text on the registration screen of its sequel, *Caverns of Kroz*:

> This is not a shareware game, but it is user-supported. If you enjoy this game you are asked by the author to please send a registration check in the amount of $7.50 to Apogee Software. This registration fee will qualify you to order any of the other Kroz volumes available. . . . [A list of Kroz games follows.]
>
> . . . Each game is priced $7.50 each, any three for $20 or all six for only $35. You'll also get a secret code that makes this game easier to complete, plus a "Hints, Tricks and Scoring Secrets" guide and "The Domain of Kroz" map.

As an aside, it's remarkable that pretty much the same principle of added downloadable content and secret codes unlocking unique objects is at play now, as the idea of extending a game beyond a disk (or download) to a more dynamic, active relationship with the consumer becomes the norm. This is reason alone for Miller to be recognized as playing an enormous role in the development of business models for the games industry. It's also interesting that this Apogee model (as it is generally known) actually contributed to the design and structuring of *Wolfenstein 3D* and, subsequently, *DOOM*. It relied heavily on online distribution, which, given the constraints previously noted, meant that games had to be screwed down incredibly tight in terms of overall size. This also pushed them toward episodic structures, with the action broken into self-contained but linked units that offered an initially free but complete package while leading on to further purchases. As Kushner notes, shareware games were distributed via modem, which meant they had to be relatively small in size; they also needed to be split into discrete episodes of action, to allow players to sample free versions before committing to buy. In other words, shareware more or less inevitably pushed any developer interested in the model toward not only arcade-style gaming but also some kind of rolling story or Intellectual Property (IP) that would naturally extend beyond the free segment into the monetized one(s). Large interwoven role-playing games just weren't going to work; the sense of completeness of the free section of the game was critical. As Hall points out, "People were kinda iffy on demos, but getting a whole game, then two more if you register was a great incentive" (THa). Ford made a similar argument, noting that what really made the Apogee model work is that the free games were "complete and playable," as opposed to "some programmers' attempts to cripple their software to force payment, leaving users frustrated and angry" (Ford 2000).

id had adopted the Apogee model (or been adopted by Apogee, depending on how you look at it) from *Keen* to *Wolfenstein 3D,* and there was a fair bit of anticipation for *DOOM*, built by leaked alphas and the occasional hyperbolic press statement. When *DOOM* hit, everything was set to send it stratospheric, assuming, of course, that the product was right. Although Mäyrä is right that *DOOM* was slotting into pop culture in a particularly well-timed way, I'm not sure he gives the game enough credit when he argues it should not be seen "as an isolated incident in the history of digital games" (2008, 103). The shareware model, the rise of the Internet, pop-culture links to films like *The Evil Dead* and *Aliens,* and the heavy metal scene certainly added fuel to the fire. Cloud attributes a measure of *DOOM*'s success to being in the right place at the right time, at least as far as shareware's capacity to bypass publishers and get more idiosyncratic visions directly into the hands of the target market, a process we have seen repeated in the recent indie explosion.

> And of course, we were in a very lucky spot with this whole shareware craziness. Creativity has a chance to grow through the concrete, and you get small teams of guys out there kicking ass and doing some very cool things. And that's where shareware gave an opportunity to a handful of guys who wouldn't have been able to put together a proposal for a publisher for the life of us. . . . We could get together, put something out, and if people like it, they sent us a check. Worked out. In a different time, that would have been a challenge to do. (KC)

But it's doubtful whether a weaker game would have achieved the extraordinary impact of *DOOM*. Romero, while reinforcing how important shareware was, argues that the technology (manifesting most vividly through the visuals) and the sheer speed of *DOOM* went a long way toward wowing the crowd. When he says that "the greatest game that anyone had played . . . was FREE—that was huge, huge, huge," the fact that *DOOM* arguably *was* the greatest game anyone had played was the deciding factor. Carmack concurs with this estimation, arguing that *DOOM* was one of the first games to break out of the ghetto and achieve a visibility outside the closed world of gamers and geeks. For him, this ties back to the discussions of virtual reality that had a degree of visibility in the public domain: *DOOM* actually seemed to be delivering what had previously only been theorized about, promised, or represented in a movie. He describes it as a "critical threshold of presentation" (JC). There was also the brilliant notion of allowing anyone to sell the shareware version of *DOOM* retail, rather than just relying on online distribution. Romero elaborates,

> When we were marketing *DOOM*, the reason why the title screen on *DOOM* says suggested retail price $9.99 was because we told everybody that could put the shareware version of *DOOM* in a box in any store that they could keep all the money. We didn't want any money, we just wanted the game in a box in a store. So when you went to the store back then, in the United States at least, you could see ten boxes of *DOOM* on the same shelf, and they'd all be from different manufacturers in different boxes, but they all had the same thing in them. (JR)

DOOM exploded. For obvious reasons, it's impossible to track the actual distribution of the shareware version. We've already seen claims of more than ten million installations, and VGChartz estimates 2.85 million units for the PC version, although this may include the 1995 retail release of *Ultimate Doom*. Tellingly, even id has no idea exactly how many units were eventually sold.

Critically, DOOM was an instant hit, racking up an impressive array of awards. In 1994, it won Game of the Year from *Computer Gaming World,* both Game of the Year and Game Innovation at the European Computer Trade Show, Technical Excellence awards from *PC Magazine,* Best Action Adventure from the Academy of Interactive Arts and Sciences, and Best Sound and Music from *MegaGames.* It was a reader's choice finalist for *Multimedia World*'s Best Action Arcade award in 1995 and was the runner-up for Action Game of the Year from *Strategy Plus* in 1994 (beaten at the post by a relative unknown called *DOOM II*). It also picked up the Best Overall Product Franchise award from *Videogame Advisor* in 1996.

Members of the press were ecstatic. "Four letters, one syllable and a major international phenomenon. Never before has a computer game gathered such a cult following" was Jeffrey Adam Young's take on things in the December 1994 issue of *Video Games* magazine. "Never a dull moment . . . we want more," gushed *PC Format,* giving the game a rating of 92 percent and a *PCF* Gold Award. *Computer Gaming World* was left in no doubt either. Bryan Walker's 1994 review is the breathless rave of a true believer.

> *DOOM* is a virtuoso performance. Stunning graphics, pulse-pounding sound, intense gameplay, and multiplayer mayhem combine to form what is probably the best action game to date.

Walker puts in the kind of reviewer's complaint that developers can only dream about.

> The resulting adrenaline surge, mixed with the tremendous suspense of the hunt, actually caused me to break my cherished Thrustmaster joystick! That's how intense multiplayer *DOOM* can get!

He then notes reports of deathmatch getting banned at various corporations—at which point an editor's note suggests it's on the verge of being banned at *CGW*. Elsewhere, Denny Atkins of *Compute!* was being seduced by the game despite himself.

> No computer game you've ever seen has graphics and sound like this. Three-dimensional texture-mapped buildings, the smoothest scrolling you've ever seen, and tension-building sound effects draw you into *DOOM*'s reality. The game is ultraviolent, with monster guts splattered throughout the levels as you play. I hesitantly admit feeling a perverse sense of pleasure when I figured out how to make a monster's guts actually bespatter the walls. This isn't the game to let your children play when you're trying to teach them the evils of violence, as *DOOM* definitely glorifies it. (Atkins 1994)

It's customary to talk at this point about the controversy that surrounded the game, although it's not something I particularly want to dwell on, partly because this book is about the game itself, rather than how it got co-opted into political battles, and partly because doing so means trotting out material that's already been covered at some length. The short version is that *DOOM* launched at about the same time that political momentum was already building to do something about violence in the media and particularly in games. Seventeen years later, this appears to be something of a cyclical pattern, despite the interim period producing no convincing evidence of any short- or long-term harmful effects of playing games. *Wolfenstein 3D* had already raised a few hackles with its Nazi blasting antics, so as new graphics upped the ante in terms of what the *DOOM* Bible called "beefy chunklets" or orbs of innard, it was no surprise *DOOM* would be swept along in the hysteria. It's important to note, as Kushner (2003, 153–58) points out, that antigaming rhetoric had been kicking around since the early 1980s, but the timing of *DOOM*'s release was spectacular, arriving roughly twenty-four hours after Senator Joseph Leiberman issued a demand to the games industry to start rating games or face government intervention, on the grounds of violence and addiction ruining the world (again). As Denny Atkins put it,

> If Congress is concerned now about the level of violence in electronic entertainment, let's hope nobody mails a copy of *DOOM: Knee-Deep in the Dead* to Capitol Hill. This latest blastfest from id Software (creator of *Wolfenstein 3-D*) is a graphic extravaganza that's completely free of the kinds of redeeming societal values found in SimHealth—unless you can find social value in cutting up mutant undead soldiers with a chain saw. (Atkins 1994)

DOOM's creators were and remain more or less nonplussed about controversy over the violent content of the game. Jay Wilbur shrugged off the question in *Video Games* magazine.

> That only comes up when the press asks about it. The public don't care. I haven't been in contact with politicians other than to know that people on The Hill [Capitol Hill, where Congress sits] are playing it. I don't believe in censorship, but I wouldn't oppose something that states *DOOM* is violent. (Young 1994)

Carmack was happier to engage with the debate but remembers being assigned minders to "kick him" if he started to discuss the subject with journalists. He says his position has always been that he is "happy to offend the easily offended." Both he and Cloud maintain that an important point not usually dwelt on is that the *DOOM* player is the hero; there are none of the moral ambiguities of *Grand Theft Auto III* (DMA Design 2001), *Fallout 3*, or even *Fable III* (Lionhead Studios 2010).

In our games you always were the hero. You know, you're supposed to be defending humanity against the forces of evil. You're not going to go and pull a Gandhi against the forces of Hell; you want your heavy armaments. (JC)

In any case, the debate over games and violence is one for another time and place, short of noting that *DOOM*'s brand of cartoon gore and Satanism-lite ensured that it entered pop culture as a controversial entity even for those who had never played it or had any intention of playing it. For those who did play, the spread of the shareware version was extraordinary, with the networked multiplay aspect of the game threatening to make true id's claim to be the "number one cause of decreased productivity in businesses around the world." Kushner reports that Intel and Carnegie Mellon, among other organizations, banned the game due to system load problems.

I've made the case that id, if not actually unique, was comprised of a pretty uncompromisingly focused development team in a very special place and with a very special mind-set. We've seen how *DOOM* grew naturally from the world of *Wolfenstein 3D* and beyond, back through a long and important tradition of first-person gaming. I've discussed how it mutated and changed through its development, and I've shown how this was supported by technology that was genuinely groundbreaking. All of this sets the scene. Now it's time to actually get our hands covered with gunpowder and entrails and to examine, in a bit more detail, "the greatest game ever made."

CHAPTER 8

A "Shot-by-Shot" Analysis of *DOOM*, Part 1

Knee Deep in the Dead

You're standing in some kind of entrance hall. There are open windows, and you can see mountains in the distance. There's a carpet area, a barrel. Out of a hole in the wall to the right, you can see a courtyard with a pool of green gunk in which there's a glowing armor suit. Off to the left, an antechamber has a set of stairs leading up to green armor on a plinth. There are some helmets and blue vials about. Your hand, holding a frankly quite small pistol, sits above a HUD, the centerpiece of which is a chisel-jawed hardass with a crew cut, looking pensively from left to right. You fire a shot from the pistol, which jerks up with the recoil; somewhere in the distance, something yowls in response. Welcome to the Phobos Base.

All right, then. Let's dispense with the story first, as it's not going to take too long in the grand scheme of things. According to the game's manual,

> In *DOOM*, you're a space marine, one of Earth's toughest, hardened in combat and trained for action. Three years ago you assaulted a superior officer for ordering his soldiers to fire upon civilians. He and his body cast were shipped to Pearl Harbor, while you were transferred to Mars, home of the Union Aerospace Corporation. The UAC is a multi-planetary conglomerate with radioactive waste facilities on Mars and its two moons, Phobos and Deimos. With no action for fifty million miles, your day consisted of suckin' dust and watchin' restricted flicks in the rec room.

For the last four years the military, UAC's biggest supplier, has used the remote facilities on Phobos and Deimos to conduct various secret projects, including research on inter-dimensional space travel. So far they have been able to open gateways between Phobos and Deimos, throwing a few gadgets into one and watching them come out the other. Recently however, the gateways have grown dangerously unstable. Military "volunteers" entering them have either disappeared or been stricken with a strange form of insanity—babbling vulgarities, bludgeoning anything that breathes, and finally suffering an untimely death of full-body explosion. Matching heads with torsos to send home to the folks became a full-time job. Latest military reports state that the research is suffering a small setback, but everything is under control.

A few hours ago, Mars received a garbled message from Phobos. "We require immediate military support. Something fraggin' evil is coming out of the gateways! Computer systems have gone berserk!" The rest was incoherent. Soon afterwards, Deimos simply vanished from the sky. Since then, attempts to establish contact with either moon have been unsuccessful.

You and your buddies, the only combat troops for fifty million miles were sent up pronto to Phobos. You were ordered to secure the perimeter of the base while the rest of the team went inside. For several hours, your radio picked up the sounds of combat: guns firing, men yelling orders, screams, bones cracking, then finally silence. Seems your buddies are dead.

Things aren't looking too good. You'll never navigate off the planet on your own. Plus, all the heavy weapons have been taken by the assault team leaving you only with a pistol. If only you could get your hands around a plasma rifle or even a shotgun you could take a few down on your way out. Whatever killed your buddies deserves a couple of pellets in the forehead. Securing your helmet, you exit the landing pod. Hopefully you can find more substantial firepower somewhere within the station. As you walk through the main entrance of the base, you hear animal-like growls echoing throughout the distant corridors. They know you're here. There's no turning back now.

There are no cutscenes in *DOOM*. The story doesn't intrude any further into the action beyond loosely theming the levels and bolting the three episodes together with a bit of linking text. So we can take the core pegs from the backstory: it's Hell in there; you're on your own; you're underequipped and outnumbered; whatever is going on, it's kind of UAC's fault one way or another (shades of the corporate conspiracies of *Aliens*); and you are a kick-ass loner who likes to shoot first and ask questions later, albeit a moralistic one. So don't be expecting any diplomacy in what follows.

While *DOOM*'s story could be criticized for being fairly crude, that would be missing the point. A more interesting way of thinking about story in games than getting all riled about narrative sophistication or comparative analysis with other media forms is to stick to the question of story's purpose or function. *DOOM* may not be literature, but as a functional tool for supporting gameplay, it's absolutely spot on. When we think about plot in stories, it makes more sense to think of it as being a reductive process, rather than additive. We tend to conceive of plot as being a causal sequence: this happens because that happened, which happened because that happened, and so on and so on, with progression in world, character, and so forth until the credits roll. In the meantime, we've carved out a nice dramatic arc. However, what is also going on is that our expectations and interpretations of these causal sequences are being steered, managed, and, critically, reduced. Details of the story work to influence our expectations and understandings of events. When we discover that Gandalf is a wizard in J. R. R. Tolkien's *The Lord of the Rings* (1954–55), a whole set of preexisting understandings about what that might mean swings into play and helps us contextualize his actions accordingly, making the action make sense and stopping us from expecting things that are not going to happen. In other words, we know that Frodo is a Hobbit, which means that when he is faced with a tall door with a high handle, we don't spend our time thinking, "That's unrealistic. Why doesn't he just open it?" We know he's going to have to find a box to stand on first. Games have always suffered a little from trying to stop players from wanting to do obvious actions that the system doesn't support, and story is a particularly good way of not so much hiding this but giving the player a tidy, useful get-out clause when faced with a dissonance between what the game allows and what a reasonable action might be.

Story in games is arguably focused on this target of expectation management and contextualization (apart from the equally valid function of being something to read about on the back of the box). It can be used to help us accept the world, or *diegesis,* that the game presents. In the case of *DOOM*, it helps limit the expectations of what we might find and how we might be allowed to react (in terms of supported actions), focusing and driving gameplay. Everybody's dead: don't expect to find other people to talk to.

There's no talking, no need for social artificial intelligence, no need to worry about intricacies of plot, no worries about what choices we might have to make. Everything that moves wants to kill us and is a brainless, hate-filled, bloodthirsty aberration and an insult to God and man: shoot anything that moves (unless you can chainsaw it instead). Enjoy the slaughter. Remember, you are an honorable man (you socked that civvy-killing coward of an officer), and this is not just about saving the world; it's about revenge. A weird hellish dimension is leaking into this universe, which means anything goes. So if we want to dump a castle built of kidneys into the middle of a toxic waste refinery, that's just the way it goes here in Hell. Given that the bases have been sucked into Hell and warped and twisted and eviscerated by the process, if we miss a few details about normal, expected life, that's just what happens when you rip stuff out of one dimension and dump it into another.

This might all sound a little crass, but it's actually quite important. *DOOM*'s backstory gives you a solid, robust framework for settling into a well-defined set of expectations about just what's going to happen for the next few hours, how you need to respond, and what the system is going to give you in response. It's a contract, and it's a very well-honed one. Ironically, in the world of contemporary shooters, *DOOM*'s simplicity stands up really well. We're not going to have that near-the-end rush of exposition, extrapolation, and unconvincing connectivity as plot and character elements are hurriedly thrown together to make some semblance of dramatic conclusion or sense. We're not going to have to try and avoid the fact that our superintelligent scientist opted to shoot his way through four gazillion heavily armed exoskeletal shock troopers rather than just using his world-saving brain to reprogram the landing coordinates of the pandimensional fleet to have them miss the Earth altogether. We won't have a combined technomagical force field enslaving the whole of humanity, kettling them into a killing zone called Earth, able to be sabotaged with the touch of one button, just like pulling the plug . . . Oh wait, that's *DOOM II*. Look, the point is that you know what you are getting in *DOOM*, and the game can just sit back and concentrate on delivering. We will be expected to run and shoot and run and shoot, until there are no more corridors and no more demons. Then we will win, and they will lose. Regardless of the increase in sophistication of both artificial intelligence and world spinning, as the dominant drivers of story in games, *DOOM*'s lean, mean, storytelling machine still stands as a beacon of how to do it.

id doesn't hold back in the opening seconds of *DOOM*: we get the full impact of the new engine's capabilities right there in front of us. The cut-through sectors give you a glimpse of a huge exterior space, which pushes the variable height into a whole new dimension. Slightly more subtly, the entrance lobby contains a drop-down central carpeted area and is distinctly nonsquare in shape. Off to the left, there is a staircase to a smaller room, with pillars breaking the space around this into more complex shapes. The color palette of browns and grays shouts a level of realism that *Wolfenstein 3D* didn't get anywhere near. A barrel positioned temptingly in the center of the screen just aches to be shot at and delivers a meaty crunching explosion that scatters debris across the screen. There's a puddle of beefy chunklets in the center of the carpet and a body beyond that. The lights vary in this room—we can see the light from the large window to the right. When we pause by this window, the open areas seem huge, and we can see a lake of animated green goo. A glowing piece of armor sitting in the lake tells us straightaway that we can leave the corridors and rooms and actually get outside. Right across the lake, there's another window and a distant figure. We fire experimentally and hear him roar far off and then fire right back. Bobby Prince's crunching rock soundtrack kicks in. We skirt around to the left toward the pillars (which are throbbing and glowing with light) and head up the staircase to a plinth with animated scrolling textures, to collect some armor. On the way, a shaven-headed goon with a shotgun bellows at us. We fire, and he flies backward in a gush of blood, dropping the shotgun. We collect it and scoop up some blue health vials and some archaic metal helmets for an armor bonus, and we're ready to go. *DOOM* doesn't bother with gentle introductions; we're straight into the action.

Other innovations introduced in the first level include multiple vertical levels included in the same area. In the third room we enter, Imps stand on a raised platform in the far corner, while Zombie soldiers advance along a walkway that zigzags over green radioactive waste. There are a number of linked secrets, establishing that opening up new areas involves not just finding and triggering buttons and trip wires but triggering things in sequence. In this case, we have a different-colored wall panel, dropping down into a passage that takes us to the lake of waste with the superarmor, then a trip wire in the final room that lowers the Imp platform, announcing dynamic vertical-level adjustment and opening up a little area with a shotgun and shells. Finally, moving back out of this area and toward the second room opens a timed lift in the corner of the secret shotgun area, which we can run back to before it raises again (and it only does this once; some secrets are nonrepeatable). The lift leads to a short corridor with a couple of small armor bonuses before delivering the real reward, a one-way wall with a view over the walkway room. In the space of a few short and small secrets, the game trains the observant player or completionist to watch for wall discoloration, lines of light/shadow and new sectors as trip wires, raising and dropping platforms, and linked sequences.

Hangar is a short level, a rapid-fire introduction to the world and gameplay. According to the par times (i.e., the target time to complete the level) given at the end of each level, a great example of a cheap and simple feature that bolts on an entirely new form of replay, the goal is thirty seconds. The fact that this par becomes increasingly difficult as the game progresses adds weight to Romero's claims about the importance of skill in playing *DOOM*. To achieve a par speed requires real dexterity, of a different kind than that needed to survive the Nightmare difficulty level.[1] In fact, speedrunning became such a phenomena that you can still find archives out there collating videograbs of the very best, and they really are quite extraordinary to watch. Over on the DooMed Speed Demos Archive, for example, we can see Radek Pecka clear all four episodes on Nightmare difficulty in just over forty minutes[2] and Thomas "Panter" Pilger clearing the Hangar in a giddy nine seconds.[3] This culture was enabled by the game's capacity to record play. This, along with the obsessive and vocal character of *DOOM*'s fan base, ensured that the top speedrunners, like clans and modders, were minor celebrities in their own right. Speedruns developed their own vocabulary, with different formats requiring different ways of clearing the level. UV Max, for example, requires the player to hit 100 percent of kills and secrets on Ultra Violence before exiting the level, as opposed to UV Speed, where surviving to the exit as fast as possible is all that is required. Then there are "Tyson" runs, where the player only has access to fists and a pistol but is still required to rack up 100 percent of kills. The list goes on. Annual awards such as Compet-n gave speedrunners a platform and everyone else a focus point to check out the crazies and feel slightly inadequate about their own attempts to hit par.

In the meantime, we've stumbled out of the Hangar and into the Nuclear Plant, where we share the stage with none other than Bill Gates, who was superimposed onto this level complete with trench coat, shotgun, and chunky wool knit cardigan for a promo video screened at a Windows 95 event, promising support for "games like these."[4] Seriously. And next time your PC crashes, just think, "Don't interrupt me!" In E1M2, the complexities the new engine allowed are really let off the leash by Romero, in a much larger and more complicated setup. While the texturing is still predominantly sci-fi industrial (we really don't start seeing heavy gothic, pseudomedievalist architecture until Sandy Peterson's work starts making its presence felt in Episode 2), there's a wide spread of lighting styles and environments. The first room is a large space, with a split-level central room-within-a-room, complete with lift and strobing lights. A sweeping staircase arcs around the room, joining at a high level corridor that makes the most of *DOOM*'s ability to give the impression of vertically stacked environments even when the sensation was cheated and the sectors actually lay side by side. A short open-air environment can be opened with a secret door, and we find our first keycard, starting the process of hunting and doubling back that still characterizes most linear shooters today. Leaving the first large room, we find ourselves in the dark corridors that, more than anything else, are classic *DOOM* environments. Off to the right, a dismal nukage-filled chamber hides a button on a pillar that will open the first genuinely terrifying section: a small maze of computer banks stocked with Troopers and Imps that is, to a large extent, either strobe-lit or not lit at all. This section, where there are plenty of places for Imps to hide, is where sound flooding really comes into its own. The first shot fired provokes a chorus of snarls and hisses, and the only way forward is into the flickering dark. Do you hold your breath and edge slowly forward or just make a run for it?

Buried in the dark (in this part of the map that is nonessential, which is extraordinary given its scale) are some goodies: a chainsaw and a backpack. But it's not just the tangible rewards that pull you in: the real point of subjecting yourself is the thrill of the scare and the rush of the battle. Exploration is encouraged by a much easier "secret" area along the main spine of the level. We can ignore the nukage/button room and the dark maze and plough on up the stairs toward the exit, but there's a very obvious drop-away lift that sends you down to a room with a window to the chainsaw area. Again, we are being offered the opportunity to charge through the levels or to move more slowly and unlock all the secrets. This idea of minor deviations from a central spine are core design tactics for nearly all linear shooters. Arguably, *DOOM* is responsible for that, which represents another massive contribution to the genre, if not the medium.

On we go toward the Toxin Refinery, which has the most complex sequence of secret sections so far. Once again the level presents a fast, linear solution coupled with a much larger exploratory area, which culminates in opening up a new section that ultimately leads to a bonus secret level.

It also builds further the complexity of vertical scale. This is evident from the donut-shaped exterior section that includes not just a walkway across a deep drop to nukage but an Imp sniping from a higher corridor and a complex system of rooms in the secret section, which are visible from the central corridor. To access these, we must run through the first secret area in time to catch a lowering and raising wall that provides access to a hidden area containing a rocket launcher. The room with the rocket launcher also contains a nukage-filled tunnel leading to a switch that raises a bridge crossing from the very first room to a brick wall, which is actually a hidden door. Also running off the first secret area is a second dropping wall section that spirals down the stairs to a room with a Soul Sphere on a pillar, visible from the corridor just off the player start point. The exploring player has a choice between the two exits, one leading on to E1M4 Command Control, the other, via the newly opened bridge secret, to the bonus level E1M9 Military Base. Let's detour through the latter first.

E1M9 swaps a straightforward linear design with nonessential side areas for a more hub-and-spoke approach, with four major rooms branching off a central open-air location (fig. 10). At the center of this is what appears to be a large cage, packed full of Imps. This is one of the potential indications that there is slightly more story going on than first appears, as it would seem that the UAC is actually aware of the Hellish denizens. This is, of course, now a standard aspect of the average FPS story, where the simple fact of invasion by alien or supernatural forces is given more flavor by the added conspiracy of dark forces within the military-industrial complex. *Half-Life* really trades off this idea, with black ops units being sent in to massacre the Black Mesa scientists and cover up the attack (in the We've Got Hostiles level), the discovery of labs to experiment on Xen aliens (in the Questionable Ethics level), and, finally, the use of the human teleport devices to reach the Nihilanth at the end of the game. In *DOOM*'s case, it's entirely questionable whether or not the average player will pick up on this subtle subplot. To be honest, only when seeing it mentioned on a forum as I was doing the rounds for this book did it cross my mind that the structure at the center of E1M9 was actually a "cage" used to "imprison" Imps. You live and learn.

Anyway, there are a couple of additional things in E1M9 we should pick up on. First, in a room to the northeast of the base, which is open and available from the start (which means, given that a large proportion of the base is locked down, it's highly likely to be found by the player), there is a pentacle of glowing red material on the floor, a candle at each corner, and a very

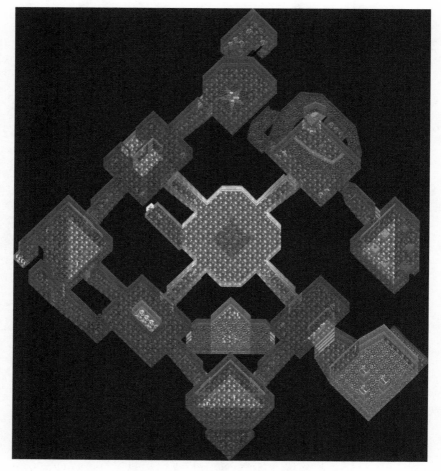

Fig. 10. The hub design of *DOOM*'s E1M9 Military Base.
(From Ian Albert, www.ian-albert.com/doom_maps.)

tempting missile launcher in the center. We'd have to be the most naive of players—not to mention probably to have slept through the previous three levels—not to smell a trap, but this is *DOOM,* we're playing it, and trap or no trap, we want that new gun. As soon as we grab it, however, *DOOM* lets rip with a new trick: teleporters. These days, teleporting around a level or using teleporters as a means of dumping monsters into any spawn point (without, frankly, needing to justify it at all) is old hat, but here we're seeing it for the first time, and it is quite a first time. With a series of green flashing sprites, the room fills with Pinkys, Imps, and Troopers, and all hell breaks loose. The monsters are being piped in from a room sitting just next door to this one, without a connecting door but with a direct portal turned on by the trip switch of the player picking up the launcher. Interestingly, we only find a teleporter on two other occasions in Episode 1. There is a pentacle in another secret area in E1M5 Phobos Lab that doesn't really do much apart from add some intrigue and send us back to the start. The other is found in basically the very last moment of the episode, following the defeat of the Barons, but we'll come to that in due course. In Episodes 2 and 3, however, teleporters play a much more active role, including maps that are built around them as a central mechanic in E2M1 Deimos Anomaly, E3M5 Unholy Cathedral, and E3M7 Gate to Limbo.

The second design point we should mention is the first (and, in reality, only) bit of platforming in *DOOM*, which takes place in a secret area just off the exit room. In here, we're presented with a series of pillars with items perched on top of them. At the far end of the room, a raising section is triggered by the player's entrance. From the top of this, it's possible, by sprinting and making sudden stops or turns, to make it from pillar to pillar, snatching up choice items such as a chainsaw, ammo, and a backpack. It's actually very tricky to get this right, and it is interesting that it's the only time a player has to do anything like it in all three episodes. Once FPS games added in a jump feature, platforming became more popular (although it is somewhat out of favor again, *Mirror's Edge* notwithstanding). Certainly, Romero didn't consider that it could be supported as a common feature of gameplay.

> I just put those platforms in there as the ultimate torture. Since you couldn't look down, it made the running and "jumping" really difficult. It was just there to give the player a tough challenge and reward. In *DOOM II*, the player encounters this in level 2. I didn't want to include it in any mainstream areas of the game, because it just wasn't fair, since jumping wasn't supported and you couldn't see your feet. I loved *Half-Life*'s Xen level and its jumping. If I have good jumping and air control in a game, I have no problem with jumping on ledges. (JR)

It is clear is that over the course of Episode 1, Romero was systematically testing the design potential of the engine, not just with teleporters and platforming but through the use of strobing lights, exterior areas, multiple trip wires, sequenced monster closets, cut-through sectoring, and linked set piece. Essentially, as he added "world interactive elements (strobe lights, switches, platforms, stairs rising/falling, et cetera)," this was defining both the order and nature of the levels he designed. In other words, we can get a sense of the order in which features and functions were added to DOOM by checking them against the order in which Romero remembers making the levels: E1M2 around April 1993, then E1M5, E1M3, E1M6, E1M1, E1M7, and E1M9 (with Petersen building E1M8 at around the same time as E1M7).

Hall shares credit with Romero on E1M4 Command Control (he worked on it around June 1993), which is interesting as a level clearly divided into two major areas, each of which allows for a much more open choice of approach than previous levels. The center point is a large circular chamber containing the blue key needed to access the second half of the level. This is reached via one of three possible paths: a short run through a more or less empty room, a battle with Troopers and Pinkys in a larger computer lab with a tall upper walkway, or a darker nukage area with Imps and a chance to rack up a few extra items by running along the river of damaging guck. Whichever path is taken, we end up releasing a whole bunch of Imps from inside the circular chamber, picking up a chaingun and the blue keycard, and opening up the second part of the level. There are two initial directions to head in, although the level is actually linear from here on in. We can shortcut to the exit, via a blue computer room that, at a trigger, actually drops all of its inner walls[5] to release a bunch of monsters who have been perched atop them, but we'll be faced with a set of stairs that leads to an exit yet has a section of floor missing. To actually get to this, we need to hit the first proper maze section in the game, although it's probably worth stating that this isn't a maze under any real definition of the term. It's not exactly hard to find our way through it. The point is more that we've moved from open corridors, where we could see stuff (Pinkys, fireballs, that kind of thing) heading in our direction from a way off and honed our strafing skills to avoid getting hit. Suddenly we're in tiny, cramped, poorly lit corridors, without the time or space to do either. Just like platforming, this abrupt change of environment forces a different gameplay style, where even hardened players are forced to push forward slowly, then backpedal furiously, firing as they go. Either way, the button to raise the floor section lies at the end of the maze and then it's straight on to E1M5 Phobos Lab.

Here, the level is based around two large set-piece areas with a third tucked away at the end of the level. The use of split-levels and windows ramps up here as well. The first large open area is a walkway around a nukage pit, which is overlooked by a small office room, and both are accessible from the opening area. It's possible to snipe monsters in the open area from a window here, and the other exit of the room looks out over another nukage pit, with an inaccessible door set further along the wall. To get at this, another route off the opening area leads to a projecting vantage point over the room (another window), which triggers a walkway being raised from the nukage to allow the player to gain entry to the previously denied door. Inside here, we find another small room with another window, allowing the player to empty a room of monsters previously undiscovered, in relative safety. Once again, exploration gives rewards. The forced route through the level requires the player to travel through the first open area to the second set piece. Here, a lift drops the player into a curving horseshoe staircase with Imps sniping from high-level vantage points to either side. The horseshoe surrounds another nukage pool with a switch on the far side, and two pillars, which drop monsters into the room and then raise once (but just the once, meaning a choice must be made), enabling the fast player to access some items. Reaching the nukage pool also opens two large monster closets, and the switch itself opens a door across the nukage in the first large open section, leading the way to the back part of the level. Opposite the switch in the second set piece is a secret door, leading to a tiny area with another secret door, which leads to the large exterior environment visible through windows in the preceding room and a bonus. Again, we don't see this kind of supersmall, superfast, sequenced secrets again in the game, until possibly the strange final section of E3M4 House of Pain, and it feels once more like Romero is playing with design, seeing what the engine can do and how it works.

What's really impressive about the entirety of Episode 1 is that it doesn't settle into a few brilliant tricks. There's an evolution of environment and a focus on particular aspects of its capabilities in each level, making them feel, for me at least, slightly more varied than Episode 2 (although it does feel as if Petersen is engaging in a parallel, if quite different, process of design exploration in Episode 3). Once again, this is quite probably due to the simultaneous evolution of the engine, tools, and functions alongside the level and gameplay design.

The final set piece of E1M5 is a large room full of monsters, which would be fine if it weren't for the fact it is very, very dark. A pulsing strobe light means the action is staccato and panicky, and this feels like the first time Romero really pushes the dynamic lighting id Tech 1 enabled as a *design tool* to create unique gameplay rather than just an atmospheric *art tool*. Prior to this, we've had the terrifying "Lights off! Monster closet open!" moment in E1M3 when grabbing a keycard, but suddenly we're confronted with a large, confusing area already full of howling monsters we have to plunge into. Tension was, of course, as much a trademark of *Wolfenstein 3D* as was slaughtering Nazis, but the only way you couldn't anticipate what was up ahead was if it was around a corner or beyond a door. The kind of set piece E1M5 offers at its close established a template that the overwhelming majority of FPS games since have drawn on at some point. In this one dark room, the seeds are sown for *S.T.A.L.K.E.R.: Shadow of Chernobyl*'s terrifying X-Labs (GSC Game World 2007) and, of course, for the pitch-black tunnel crawls of *DOOM 3* (id Software 2003).

By caricaturing Phobos Lab as the "set-piece" level, I do not mean to underplay the importance of set pieces elsewhere in Episode 1 or *DOOM* as a whole. There are plenty of other examples, and there are even whole levels based around singular concepts (such as E3M9, which I'll discuss in much more detail later on), but Phobos Lab is a very striking case of three very distinct areas linked together. In contrast, although we can break E1M6 Central Processing into the "maze" area, the Red Key Trap Room and the Final Big Chamber of Horrors, these areas flow into one another in a way that feels distinct to the more 1-2-3 setup of its predecessor. Central Processing is Trap City: it packs more monster closets per square inch of level design than most titles manage to get into a full game.

As we took the detour through the Military Base, we're already familiar with the design principle that if something looks too good to be true, it probably means that there's an Imp hiding in the wall next to it, ready to rip your spine out through one of your eye sockets. Equally, we've already been subjected to the experience of keycard triggers, in E1M3. Central Processing, however, doesn't offer the choice of a bonus item or restrict itself to a couple of Imps. Sooner or later, to progress in the level, we're going to have to grab the red keycard—you know, the one in the huge, suspiciously empty room. There's none of the shock tactics of the Toxin Refinery, *DOOM* simply delivers in spades, sliding open half the walls in the place to flood the room with Troopers and Imps. If we survive that fight, it opens up the area containing the blue key card, which sits on a promontory over a nukage pit and just happens to release a Pinky and friends from the wall directly behind us (naively, we didn't have the presence of mind to approach the keycard backward). A quick trawl through another maze-like section, actually a series of interlinked crossroads over more nukage, gets us access to another keycard and the final big room of the level. Or so it would seem. In fact, Romero pulls a sly trick and positions a switch where the natural level end would be, which opens up an area to the east. This is something of a nod and a wink to the player—Romero saying, "Yeah, I know you think how this game works now, but we've still got a few tricks up our sleeves." In reality, Episode 2 was only a couple of levels away, and once Petersen started playing around, some of the expectations of how things worked went straight out of the window. In E1M6, we find that Romero had one final set of traps lurking up his sleeve. After clearing the dark, grimy final room, we are forced into releasing a whole fresh batch of enemies from a bunch of hidden areas in order to get at the exit.

The penultimate level of Episode 1, E1M7 Computer Station, is my personal favorite *DOOM* level ever (Romero's too, as it happens). It's also one of the original designs, appearing in both the 0.4 and 0.5 alphas. E1M7 is all about windows and remains quite possibly one of the most well-designed exercises in backtracking in game history (fig. 11). A river of nukage flows right through the center of the level, splitting it in two. Long windows down the corridors let us see the keycards we are going to need to get hold of and, on the other side, a clear line of sight right through to the exit room. To get there, we need to cover the ground right to the far side of the level, crossing over the nukage, then follow the path right down on the opposite side of the river, where we can see the next keycard we need lurking back near the start. We need to head all the way back there, pick it up, and then backtrack *again* to halfway through the level to open up the door into the final section. Here, we need to detour around to find a switch that is right next to a window showing us the room next to the exit this detour started from, now opened up to allow access to the exit and release a bunch of goons in the opposite direction, meaning a final backtrack is needed.

Anyone with more than a passing interest in games, particularly FPS games, will know that the gold standard for backtracking rests not with *DOOM* but with *Halo: Combat Evolved*, which takes it for the sheer audacity of running an entire level backward under a different name (there are lots of little changes, of course, but Two Betrayals uses basically the same environment as Assault on the Control Room). However, *DOOM* got there first, and if that's not an argument that holds for E1M7, then we'll get back

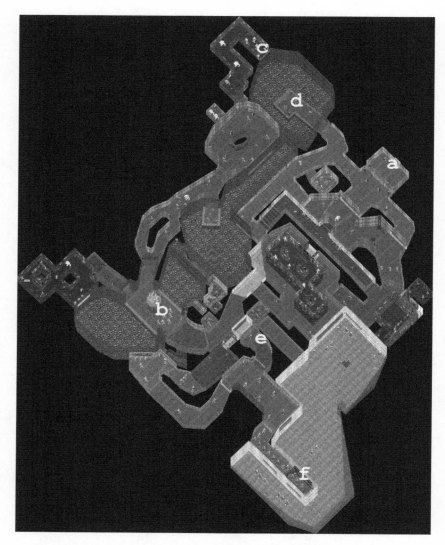

Fig. 11. *DOOM*'s E1M7 Computer Station. Players begin at point A and move through point B to point C, at which point they can return and access point D. This gives them the keycard to open E and finally reach the exit at F. The extent of the backtrack should be obvious. (From Ian Albert, www.ian-albert.com/ doom_maps.)

to the higher-than-high concept level of E3M9 in just a while. Backtracking is a bit of a dubious proposition in design, not particularly popular with players even if it's a great way of wringing the maximum possible value out of any given set of assets. Perhaps it's because *DOOM* was fairly low-resolution (although it certainly wasn't seen as low-res at the time), but the amount of backtracking in this level doesn't feel like a way of padding out gameplay without having to provide new features. Essentially, we get two and a half runs through the same environment, with new monster closets activated at the target of each run. That the monsters don't sit around waiting to be activated but actively come looking for us adds a certain edge in comparison to the first run-through, as previously "empty" rooms suddenly contain fireball-hurling Imps. Equally, the par time of the level is a mere three minutes, itself an exaggeration if Romero is to be believed (he claimed to have added thirty seconds onto his timings for each level[6] in a *PC Zone* interview in 2002). Even playing at a normal human speed, the level is probably going to be over in under fifteen minutes, which is a far cry from some of the repetitive backtracking and respawn battles of, well, *Far Cry 2* (Ubisoft Montreal 2008). In other words, the backtracking here is more succinct and doesn't outstay its welcome. Saying that is possibly a little unfair, as *Far Cry 2* has enormous rewards for the exploring player in terms of visual design and atmosphere. But, being linear, *DOOM* sculpts the backtracking experience to a far more effective degree. It's a trick that id themselves repeated in *DOOM 3*, where the entire opening section of the Mars Base is one long sequence of cascading triggers. When the player hits the end of the section and finds the scientist, triggering the invasion, a huge proportion of the level is changed, adding triggers for animations and scripted sequences, as well as new props and decals, and diverting players along alternate routes in places, as they then work their way right back to the beginning of the level again. Technically, it's a brilliant piece of design, a hugely impressive beginning to a game that, in some ways, struggles afterward to live up to this stroke of genius.

This rounds off our tour of Phobos Base, as we dive headlong into the final level of Episode 1. E1M8 Phobos Anomaly, based on an original design by Hall, is the player's first encounter with Sandy Petersen's design, and there is an instant shift in feel and flavor. The actual map itself is tiny, comprising two lead-in rooms (one full of Pinkys and barrels, basically an entertaining chain-reaction reward for making it this far) and a second small chamber with two recesses containing guns and ammo for the big finish. Beyond these is a star-shaped chamber with two big closets and two big horn-faced, goat-legged, green-fire-hurling, giant Barons of Hell, which is a cue for general panic, running around, and carnage. Barons dispatched, the entire room disappears, the walls sliding into the floors and leaving us on a star-shaped dais in an open courtyard. There's nothing to do except head for a small structure, whose stairs rise up to let us find ourselves on a platform with a giant decal of a pentacle superimposed on a satanic visage. Standing on this ends the episode and, if you were a shareware player, the game—by killing you. You are instantly teleported into a pitch-black room full of monsters who will kill you, no matter how many shots you fire. When you do bite the dust, the game throws this at you:

Once you beat the big badasses and clean out the moon base you're sup-posed to win, aren't you? Aren't you? Where's your fat reward and ticket home? What the hell is this? It's not supposed to end this way!

It stinks like rotten meat, but looks like the lost Deimos Base. Looks like you're stuck on the shores of Hell. The only way out is through.

To continue the *DOOM* experience, play The Shores of Hell and its amazing sequel, Inferno!

CHAPTER 9

A "Shot-By-Shot" Analysis of *DOOM*, Part 2

The Shores of Hell

A bunch of text appearing one character at a time over a tiled metal background is not pretty, even making allowances for it being 1993. But, then, it never really was about a glamorous final cutscene. There's a whole new episode to get through, and we're leaving behind Romero's tightly packed, visually lean and relatively logical, sci-fi design for the sprawling, lurid, and occasionally downright insane worlds of Sandy Petersen. If anything, Episode 2 functions neatly as a transition into the full gothique, as many of the levels were based on original designs and early builds by Hall. On one hand, we have the initial concept of *DOOM* and the desire to replicate "real spaces" that are evident in Hall's Bible. On the other, hitting it head-on with the meaty smack of fist into palm, are Peterson's primary colors and heavy school-of-*Cthulhu* vibe. Given that the episode's story, such as it is, is all about an industrial base sucked into Hell and warped and twisted in the process, that'd be a happy coincidence, at the very least.

Famously, Episode 2 is made up primarily of levels started by Hall and, to varying degrees, overhauled or reinvented by Petersen. This creates a unique flavor to the episode and neatly fits the concept of Hell invading the Martian bases. Petersen agrees with this idea.

> I do think that the contrast between our styles in Level 2 [*sic*] really went a long way towards making it a mix of Hell and Science Fiction. Me providing the Hell, of course. (SP)[1]

In terms of Hall's contribution, Petersen estimates that "50 percent or more" of the work was his own but credits his predecessor with "the bones" of most of it. Petersen is quick to give credit to Hall's work on "the excellent E2M2," saying that he didn't even retexture the map for the most part and that secrets and positioning were already done in the majority of cases. Petersen admits, though,

> Most of his levels were in a very primitive state when I took them on. For instance, E3M3 was one of his, but the only texture he had everywhere on the map was the silver metal one. This wasn't his fault, of course—he did that map when that was the only texture available. But I had to add a ton of stuff to complete it. (SP)

It is important to reiterate that there is no criticism of Hall's ability as a designer being made here: he simply didn't have the tools to work with at the point when he left id. The more interesting point is that if Episode 2 feels like a slightly disjointed, messy affair in places, a sense that one world is literally invading the other, then this may well come down to not just Petersen's brief of "a space station infected with Hell" but the process of early designs being overwritten and mangled to fit a new vision. It's also perhaps intriguing to note that Petersen never read Hall's Bible, that, by this point, *DOOM*'s world and concept had achieved a kind of escape velocity from much of the material it contained. I do wonder what Hell would have looked like in an alternate universe, where Hall remained and Petersen never unleashed his vision onto Deimos.

The Shores of Hell opens up with a level that wastes no time in telling us to expect something quite different. It's staccato and disjointed—seven sections of map only connected by teleporters. Gone is the type of visual orientation that Romero's use of exterior spaces and windows provided, where we could literally see where we were headed much of the time. Instead, E2M1 Deimos Anomaly offers no clues as to where we are and where we are headed (fig. 12). We may have come across teleporters in Episode 1, if we were exploring all the secret areas, so we might have a clue what these red pulsing squares are all about. But if we hit the teleporters at a run, we'll find ourselves at the end of the level without the keycards we need to get into the exit. The first of those is beyond the teleporter, off around the corner, and the second is in a secret wall we need to activate by tripping three sequential switches. Then there's this massive, red, pulsing, inverted crucifix we have

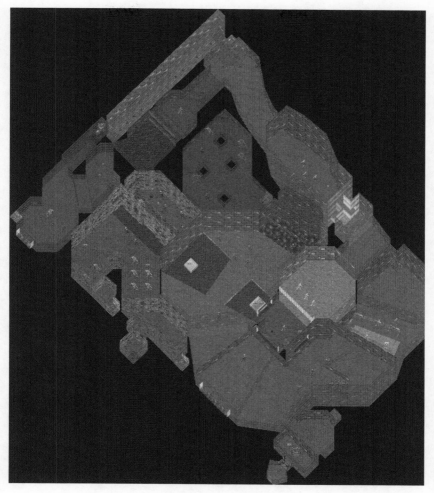

Fig. 12. Disparate map areas only linked by teleporters in *DOOM*'s E2M1. (From Ian Albert, www.ian-albert/doom_maps.)

to go through, only it hurts to do that, like a nukage floor. To begin with, it might be the normal run of gray lab walls, but two teleports later, we are in what looks like a rotting green castle. Out of the only window, we see a red sky over the mountains. Gone is the green acidic nukage; now it's rivers of blood. We get to what feels like a final room and see the switch that surely must take us forward, and then, from behind us, comes a seething, putrid hissing, and we spin round to find a huge ball of red flesh bearing down on us, spewing blue and red balls of fire.

First among the innovations of this level, teleporters fundamentally change the way in which level design can operate from this point on in *DOOM*. They immediately make clear that logical transitions in terms of moving from one sector to another are no longer necessarily the order of the day. This also frees up the design space, as the positioning of sectors is no longer quite as critical (in terms of laying spaces around one another to fake vertical stacking). Teleporters offer an easy way of faking distance, travel, and colocation and, in weaker clones to follow *DOOM*, a get-out clause for lazy or less talented designers to basically do what they want, where they want, when they want. Second, we start to see the signature fusion of sci-fi and gothic that characterizes Episode 2 and to get a real sense of the more traditional demonic stylings that Petersen was going to bring to the proceedings. Third and finally, we have not just a new monster but a new class of monster. The Cacodemon is as tall as a Baron but equally wide, a floating globe of death that dwarfs the Imps, Troopers, and Pinkys. Most important, it can fly, which offers a whole new bag of opportunities in terms of creature placement. Imps and Troopers may have been able to cross nukage spills without any problems, but they are limited in pathfinding to walkways and ledges, and drops were previously used to keep them away from the player and vice versa. Suddenly, with Cacodemons, enemies can cross chasms and drop or rise unexpectedly from gaps in the ceilings or floors. They are tough too, boasting 400 hit points and covering 93 MUS, with a lethal projectile moving at 350 MUS and inflicting 5–40 damage and with a bite dealing 10–60 damage. Yet they are vulnerable to high-rate-of-fire weapons like the chaingun and can even be pushed backward until they are unable to get a shot back.[2]

To counterbalance the Cacodemons, tucked away in a secret room in the Deimos Anomaly is a new addition to our arsenal, the Plasma Gun. This is an interesting case study of the superb weapon balancing in the game. Superficially, it's a beefed-up chaingun, firing a massive 700 shots per minute, with each shot causing 5–40 damage (that's potentially 35 extra damage per shot over the chaingun). However, balancing this is the fact that the plasma gun is a projectile (rather than hitscan) weapon, so even though the shots are fast, covering 875 MUS (in comparison, rockets travel at 700 MUS), the weapon becomes quite inaccurate at range, as target movement must be factored in. This makes the plasma gun a firm favorite in close quarters, as the rapid fire is much more likely to trigger a pain reflex in the target, reducing its ability to fight back, but the gun is compromised by limited resources and potentially severe drawbacks at range. It's this combination of factors in the weapon balance that is most critically combined with level design. In other words, inclusion of the plasma gun within a level requires reduced ammo (which can be profoundly disappointing for a player all excited about their new toy) or inclusion of areas where, like the shotgun, the weapon's capabilities are reduced. Equally, placing a rocket launcher is likely to mean any other weapon is bumped off the top spot, but it's going straight back into the holster if we suddenly hit a section of small, winding tunnels. Since *DOOM,* weapons with splash effect and projectiles like the plasma gun have become like old friends, and we all know that a shotgun is the best thing in a tight squeeze. Yet understanding how to balance shifting the player from weapon to weapon—not just providing the chance for favoritism to shine, but rewarding a dynamic, balanced, and considered approach to deploying one's arsenal—is surprisingly difficult, judging by the evidence. This is significantly more complex than *Wolfenstein 3D,* which had only one ammo counter, so the only strategy to be considered was the potential waste of bullets when sweeping an area with the chaingun.

E2M2 Containment Area is generally remembered for the large warehouse section it opens with, although that's actually only one facet of a large and complex level—even if it does take up nearly half of the actual floor plan. While, in some respects, it's not a million miles away from the claustrophobic tunnel crawls of earlier levels (in terms of fast reactions being required to cope with Imps popping up around tight bends and reduced lines of sight), the high ceiling and light, airy feel creates a quite different tone (fig. 13). Also, for the first time in the game, it is possible to climb boxes if the correct sizes are near to each other, a more sophisticated and player-friendly version of pseudoplatforming than we found in the Military Base. Give it a year or two and the addition of a jump function, and crate hopping in a beast-filled warehouse would be standard FPS fare. Once out of the warehouse, however—and it doesn't take long to get out of it—the rest of the level is a mix of gothic green castle and high-concept sci-fi, complete with blue pulsing energy tunnels, rising and falling pistons, a lava pit with a secret rising walkway, a series of five crushing ceilings, a nukage river, a sort of industrial warehouse room with a chaingun on a plinth, and a pillared area that almost resembles a high-tech jail, with incarcerated hellspawn. Containment Area also introduces two new features to the game: another

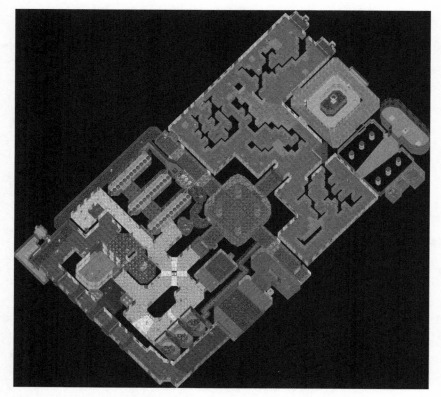

Fig. 13. *DOOM*'s E2M2 Containment Area. The box maze is the upper half of the map. (From Ian Albert, www.ian-albert.com/doom_maps.)

enemy, in the Lost Soul, and a new power-up melee weapon, Berserk. The latter fills the screen with red haze, gives an instant health boost, and increases fist damage by a factor of ten, meaning each punch now delivers a massive 20–200 damage for the remainder of the level. We still have to get up close and personal to use it, and the rate of shots per minute isn't massive, so, more than anything else, Berserk really shines as a perk for more skilled players, encouraging a more high-risk approach to combat, rather than shooting and strafing from a distance. Unlike the chainsaw, Berserk is powerful with each hit, so we don't need to stand there taking damage to do damage. In the hands of a top player, Berserk is like a cross between bare-knuckle boxing and ballet.

Lost Souls are another flying menace that subtly changes combat, as their new features mean a reconsideration of approach, particularly if they are in a mixed group (they are rarely encountered alone but are especially troublesome if it's not just Lost Souls the player is up against). Originally, way back in the press beta, the Lost Souls appeared in map 2 (which ended up as E3M5 Unholy Cathedral), still as flying skulls, but minus the flames and a hitscan attack for distance damage. By the time Episode 2 hit the streets, this was gone, replaced with a melee only attack doing 3–24 damage. Normally, the Lost Souls move at a sedate 47 MUS but are capable of a sudden charging attack, shooting toward the player at 175 MUS. On a miss, the charge carries them straight on into walls, other monsters, whatever gets in the way. They can be stopped dead with a single shot, but when a player is faced with a pack of the things, each with 100 hit points (requiring several shots to take down), the situation could very easily get out of hand. This would be amplified dramatically if the situation really called for the heavy guns, like a rocket launcher, where a premature bit of splash damage could take out even the most experienced player. In enclosed spaces, being crowded by five or six Lost Souls, all jostling for a bite, is usually an uncomfortable experience. In fact, I'd even go so far as to suggest that this is one of the very few places where *DOOM* gets it wrong. It's not a deal breaker, for sure, but while dancing around Pinkys trying to get a shot off could be tricky when they had you boxed into a corner, Lost Souls were rarely as rewarding to take on and tended more toward the irritating, forcing jerky, clumsy extrications from combat rather than enhancing the joy of the battle. Berserk was usually pretty effective against them, however, so perhaps there's no need to guess at why this weapon and enemy made their appearance in the same level.

We find ourselves in another Refinery in E2M3, which adds a few new decals and textures but provides a similar mix of environments, with a broad theme of an exterior, more vegetation-soaked base. There are a few strange additions, however, which continue to deepen the sense of Hell's grip on Deimos. For instance, in one room, we find a pink, skin-covered floor pistoning up and down, neither serving a particular gameplay purpose nor even logically fitting its surroundings. Metal walls give way to stone to creepers to wood, without any particular sense of transition. This appears to be a real example of the design tension created by Petersen working over Hall's designs. Gameplay in Refinery is also simpler than later levels such as E2M4 Deimos Lab and certainly E2M6 Halls of the Damned. There are no real traps as such; tellingly, the large room off to the left as play starts contains none of the triggered closets of, say, E1M6; it's just a big room with lots of monsters already in it. A window opposite this leads to the exit room, but its right next door, just used the once, and doesn't really have the impact of E1M7. That's not to say that Petersen/Hall are incapable of delivering complex or clever design (E2M4 Deimos Lab and E2M7 Spawning Vats are testament to that). Overall, however, this is a level stripped back to pure run-and-gun action, without much scope for exploration or the occasional simplistic puzzle.

The following level, Deimos Lab, is another thing altogether. For starters, it delivers vertical scale and distance in a way that has been absent in Episode 2 up until now. Initially, this is shown through a large chamber with a lift up to a smaller, caged area, where a secret trigger in a floor panel removes the bars and delivers a bunch of items and monsters to the player. The really key part of the first section of the level is a huge open area, comprised of a large donut-shaped central structure in a nukage lake, leading off to a series of boxlike tunnel sections. These stretch away into the distance and are open sound sectors, so we are presented with distant Imps trudging over the nukage to get to the player. To one side of this, a raised walkway can be found by taking a smaller passage, but it is not accessible at this point (though the Cacodemon perched on top of it is happy to chew the fat). We move into the box sections and, to the right, a trap room, whose entire floor lowers down, blocking a quick exit before throwing monsters at us; a crushing ceiling hides in its center. Beyond these dim walls, suddenly the level turns bright blue, like the inside of a neon-lit motherboard, and the hunt for a blue keycard to get into the second half of the level delivers both another Cacodemon and a Baron (which I strongly remember as a particularly nasty shock the first time I played DOOM, in the dark at around 4 a.m.) Then it's into the second half of the level, which centers around a large circular split-level set piece, accessed via a series of bright red chambers where the player is forced to run the gauntlet of another crushing ceiling to retrieve the yellow keycard and progress.

The circular chamber is introduced by a ring of passageways, almost joining around the far side but split by a window. A tiny crack in the floor of this passageway, which almost feels like a bug (my first reaction on finding it was disbelief that a game put together as well as DOOM could have an error as basic as a map hole) drops the player into a secret chamber with a plasma gun. Just before this, a tunnel leads down to a fiendish network of secret pas-

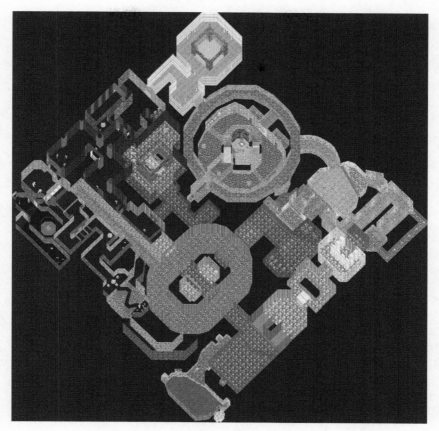

Fig. 14. *DOOM's* E2M4, showing the false vertical stack (within the large circular room at the top of the map). (From Ian Albert, www.ian-albert .com/doom_maps.)

sages, where the rewards are tempered by a couple of doors you just know are going to unload some bad Hell on you—and they duly deliver. But a skin-covered lift, complete with spinal column, delivers us way down to the floor level of the central structure, where Imps in pits are ready to usher us further on. Once this area is cleared, a pillar in the center of the room has a tunnel cut into it, with a series of switches that raise a spiral staircase back to the top (fig. 14). Given that *DOOM's* engine cannot actually stack one sector on top of another, successfully giving the sense of climbing to a higher-level room is quite impressive, and the creeper-covered stone, fleshy lifts, and subsumed computer systems effectively carry off the feeling of a weird and corrupted industrial sector. The level ends with a double-teleporter chamber and a high-level exit door, access to which requires triggering from a switch tucked away around a corner. On the way to this is a long scrolling wall of screaming faces, another step along the line of disturbing and much more gothic, supernatural, satanic, evil representations on display.

An easy mistake to fall into when looking at *DOOM*'s levels in detail is to consider their design as developed sequentially along with play, something that Petersen states emphatically was not the case (and that we've already been able to discount about Episode 1). After all, it's really tempting to see a process of refinement going on in the levels of Episode 2. E2M5 Command Center doesn't add anything particularly new to proceedings, but it's fusion of exterior and interior spaces, where players move between large open rooms and corridors to small cramped tunnels, cut-through windows, hidden rooms, and deviations to just enjoy the exploration and battling of it all, works particularly well—better (for me at least) than, say, E2M3, which equally doesn't really have any particularly outstanding features. It is important, therefore, not to get sucked into the illusion of sequential development: we know, for example, that the penultimate level of Episode 2 was actually one of the first *DOOM* levels ever designed,[3] so perhaps appreciating the design of the later levels is more about saluting Petersen's ability to sculpt experiences that are the bread-and-butter of DOOM (after all, not every level can be a concept level, and the subtleties of design that make a level great were only radical in Episode 1 because it was the first time we were seeing them in action). Command Center's rooms and corridors loop back onto themselves, and the way forward is often the least obvious door. The final run through large open corridors packed with Cacodemons is visible from a room across a by-now-familiar nukage river; elsewhere, a not dissimilar river leads around a room we've just been in, separated by a partially see-through wall of creepers, and off to a completely separate area. Hell apparently favors wood paneling too, as there's a lot of it in this level, and the sights of disemboweled, crucified, and amputated marine corpses is getting as familiar as the skull piles, sigils, and goat-headed decals.

In fact, as we've seen, the reality of the order of level construction had more to do with the developing technology of the game than anything else. Peterson explains,

> Sometimes what would happen was that John Carmack would have recently put in some new feature like teleportation, and then we'd go nuts on that theme for a while. In general I was always trying to go too far,

and they would try to rein me in. Then they'd improve the engine, and what I'd done would become acceptable. . . . I would often be working on 3–4 levels at a time or would go back to previous levels to polish or to install new monsters, treasures, textures, or special tricks that had just been made available by the programming and art teams. (SP)

This explanation is slightly different from Romero's take on things (that world functions were his responsibility, not Carmack's), and it's important to get the timeline on the game's development. Petersen joined id, initially on a month's probation in August 1993, only a couple of months before the press demo was launched, which gives an idea of the speed of production of his levels. It also perhaps doesn't give enough credit to the process of placing the levels in the final game, which fell to Romero and was followed by a process of adjusting them to make sure the game's arc was optimized. Petersen notes,

Level placement was all about the ramp: increasing complexity and size was dictating the order of the levels—simple to complex, small to big. After figuring out the level placement, tweaking the difficulty in the levels was part of the polish phase. The proper ramping of the player through the game will directly affect the game's success. (SP)

It's important to remember that the scale of the development team was comparatively small, only twelve people, which fits neatly into the more contemporary notion of a microstudio. So there was not much in the sense of a tidy development pipeline, as levels were obsessively played and played over and over again in the process of refinement. Petersen describes the process as "very informal and freewheeling."

I'd do a level and the other guys would play it and make comments. We never discarded a level, but sometimes they underwent major changes. I was responsible for naming all the monsters, for instance. I suppose there was an "approval process" in that I told the other guys about my plans, and if they didn't like something they'd tell me. . . .

I worked inside the office, and anyone was welcome to walk by and see my levels at any time. We all relentlessly played the levels and felt free to criticize even the tiniest texture choice. (SP)

Along with the sequential fallacy, the other issue Episode 2 perhaps suffers from is being the least immediately standout episode of the trilogy, and it would be a mistake to draw any conclusions about design quality from this. Everyone knowing *DOOM* knows Knee Deep in the Dead forward and backward, if for no other reason than it was the shareware episode, so most of us around in the midnineties played it to death, even if we couldn't afford the full game (I was an undergraduate at the time, so like millions of others, the shareware release got me hook, line, and sinker). Inferno contains more in the way of concept levels than either of the other two episodes, which makes many of its environments and challenges particularly memorable, from the claw-shaped map of E3E2 Slough of Despair to the striking open-air expanse of E3M6 Mount Erebus. So if there's less to say about some of these levels, that shouldn't be taken as any comment on the quality of their design. E2M6 Halls of the Damned, the very first level Petersen completed, is a good example of how wrong this would be. It's actually a fiend, deceptively complicated, and contains two of the standout moments of the episode, one of which is possibly one of my favorites of the game overall. But before we talk about that, we need to quickly mention E2M9.

The Fortress of Mystery is Episode 2's secret level, reached via a secret door in E2M5, and is basically two big rooms. One contains Barons of Hell (four of them), and the other contains Cacodemons (ten of them). As Petersen notes,

> Everyone thought it was impossible when they first played it, before they realized that monsters can be tricked into fighting other monsters. It would probably never work today, of course. (SP)

Trying to take out this armful of evil by ourselves would be absurdly challenging, but goading a big interhellspawn scrap, taking advantage of an AI blood frenzy, suddenly made the level a hugely fun experience. It's almost like a break from the action, despite the fact that we're still expected to let rip with some serious circle-strafing skills to stay in one piece. It's also quite a different feel, a self-consciously high concept built around a single set piece and requiring no exploration whatsoever. It's no accident that it arrives halfway through the episode and that the exit portal leading to it is a relatively easy secret to find. Petersen says it's his favorite level.

E2M6 starts simply enough, with the player entering into a reasonably sized room with a single doorway leading off it. So far, so ordinary. Opening the door, however, unleashes a hissing Cacodemon in a burning red room, all hellfire and brimstone. Dispatched, it leaves a switch that opens up a passage to the large exterior area that seems to sit at the center of the level. I'm always wary about reading too much into things, particularly games, but there is a lovely undertone to this, that beneath the architectural normality that makes up the undisclosed location, something more infernal is actually pulling all the strings. When the only place to go from the courtyard has two doors, one of which is the exit but requires a keycard, we may start to get the idea that this level is going to be playing with us all the way. It starts with a fairly innocuous grab of the first, blue key, opening up the inevitable shocking monster closet, but following that we hit another of those dark, strobing mazes to get the second keycard, only this maze is actually large enough to get lost in and includes the odd Pinky-infested closet. It's fairly hair-raising stuff, as there's not a great deal of room to maneuver, and we're dealing with beasts that take a few shots to put down. The final section of the level, where, presumably, we'll find the last keycard, accessed through a long tunnel, is a hub with four small, trap-filled rooms leading off it. One contains a crushing ceiling; another, four switches, each behind pumping pistons. The third seems innocuous enough, but when its door slams shut behind you, it's a yellow door, meaning there is no way out without finding the card. This is a really simple but very effective means of instantly rais-ing tension, as it's highly unlikely we're getting out of the room without a serious fight. Sure enough, a Cacodemon later and the keycard held in a bloody, triumphant fist, it's time for the last door, which, weirdly enough, is a second exit. Assuming that we didn't find the secret door behind the wall of fire in E2M5, we could be forgiven in thinking that this was the way to go. Touch the exit switch, however, and the entire floor drops away, plunging us into a room full of shotgun-wielding Troopers. It's a fantastic moment, the kind of trick you can only pull once, and it's to *DOOM*'s credit that, given the impact of the trap, its tucked away in the corner of the map, way off the beaten path.

Because of the relatively small sizes of the maps, "out of the way" in *DOOM* is never actually that out of the way, meaning that great little set pieces of design could be moved off the central spine of the level without compromising their chances of being found too badly. Perhaps there's a lesson in there for other FPS games. My favorite contemporary shooter, the Ukrainian misery fest *S.T.A.L.K.E.R.: Shadow of Chernobyl*, springs to mind as containing large quantities of superfluous but immensely reward-ing environments and set pieces, and in the first game of the franchise at least, the levels are small enough to make the exploration really rewarding. Everything in *DOOM* is only a short sprint away, and it does raise the question of whether bigger is always better in level design. Despite how wonderful sandbox shooters like *Far Cry 2* or *S.T.A.L.K.E.R.: Call of Pripyat* (GSC Game World 2010) are, there's nothing like the thrill of a well-crafted on-rails experience, which *DOOM* isn't actually so far from, in many ways. The other thing is that *DOOM* has great set pieces falling out of its pockets; it simply doesn't need every neat trick or "Oh wow!" or even "Oh no!" moment to be along the central spine. Whether it's deliberate or simply a by-product, this layout has a similar effect to using lots of white blank space in 2D visual design. It communicates a huge confidence in the product, and training the player to accept the designer's vision is an important part of gameplay. We can all think of examples where an early screwup leaves us doubting the quality of what's to come or when something has such flair and vision that you're much happier to overlook the flaws (*S.T.A.L.K.E.R.* being a prime example of that). Besides, if Petersen *et al.* were throwing away fantastic things like the fake exit, floor drop, or death room on nonessential parts of the map halfway through the three episodes, then what the Hell (literally) did they have up their gore-soaked sleeves in the levels to come?

The very first level of *DOOM* ever, that's what. Well, OK, that's not to say that it was actually the first one Romero or Hall ever bolted together, but it certainly was E1M1 of the original *DOOM* as envisaged in Hall's Bible, just arranged a slightly different way and with a handful of Petersen's magic dust sprinkled liberally into the mix. E2M7 Spawning Vats is a huge, sprawling level, an amalgamation of bits and pieces we've seen before. There's a warehouse section, only with Pinkys this time, not Imps; there's exterior nukage flows; there's a gothic castle with inverted crucifixes next door to sci-fi. But it's in the sci-fi that the level looks really quite different. It's shiny, for starters. We recognize (from the 0_4 alpha) the glossy metal walls and canisters, high-level lights, and bright blue floors. Tucked away in the middle of the map is that small, rambling staircase that comes out overlooking a metal room full of Imps, which we talked about before. And just around the corner is the Rec Room, the place it all originally started, where Lorelei Chen, John "Petro" Pietrovich, Dimitri Paramo, Thi Barrat, and, just maybe, Buddy Dacote had their card game so rudely interrupted. It's enough to make you feel all nostalgic.

Anyway, E2M7 is a sprawling level, with a less linear feel than its predecessors, and Hall's striving to create more realistic environments is almost palpable through the design. It's certainly less focused, with rooms that don't really feel like they have a great deal of purpose in terms of gameplay. They are not set pieces, leading anywhere or hosting tricks and traps or items, but that's not to say they don't work. In many ways, E2M7 is, ironically, possibly one of the most contemporary of *DOOM*'s levels, foreshadowing the age of sandboxes and more high-detail environments, when players' expect to be able to head off the beaten track and when environments are visually detailed enough to be their own goal and reward. Spawning Vats is a fun place to revisit, and I'll own up to having a real soft spot for it. It's also the last time we are going to be primarily surrounded by military-industrial sci-fi rooms and corridors, because the aesthetic of the jagged, off-kilter last room, with its switches and rising walkway over a fiery bloodbath, becomes dominant as we leave Deimos behind and head for Hell itself. First, there's the minor matter of contending with what remains one of the most infamous bosses in gaming history: the Cyberdemon of E2M8.

You're standing in a room. It's small, and there's a square plinth in the middle with a switch on each side. On each wall is the body of a chained-up, dismembered Baron of Hell. Deep breath. Hitting a switch slides open the corresponding wall, into an antechamber packed full of rockets and perhaps a couple of Lost Souls. Somewhere out there is a pounding, slamming sound: it's got to be the footsteps of something. Something big. You've made it; you are at the building that's slowly been getting bigger at the bottom of the interlevel loading screen as you've made your way through the Deimos Base. It's the Tower of Babel, and it's showdown time. E2M8 is essentially a large open space with a large structure in the center that breaks it into four sections, with three additional, smaller structures per quarter to provide cover. Once you are outside, each of the four rooms opened by the central switches is available for ammo stockpiles. Otherwise, it's just kill or be killed, a game of cat and mouse among the pillars.

Now, I'm a firm believer that it's possible to deliver material about games (and other things) in a manner that reaches all the suitable levels of scholarly robustness and factual accuracy and analytical depth and so on, without having to resort to the kind of dense, impenetrable, and jargonistic language that often plagues academic writings about media. I've been guilty of some reprehensibly convoluted theorizing in the past, and I've done my best to avoid it here, aiming instead to keep things very much in the spirit of the game and to convey a sense of what it's like to play, love, and study *DOOM*. It's in that spirit that I'd argue, with all due scholarly consideration

Fig. 15. The Cyberdemon

and objectivity, that the normal reaction to the first glimpse of the Cyberdemon guarding the Tower of Babel was a kind of keening, high-pitched
moan.

DOOM II's manual describes the Cyberdemon (fig. 15) as a "missile
launching skyscraper with goat legs," and he does, indeed, scrape the very
skybox, coming in at a massive 110 units high (twice the height of an Imp
or Trooper). He's fast, at 186 MUS (faster than a Lost Soul's charge); has a
huge 4,000 hit points, making him four times tougher than a Baron; and is
immune to splash damage, so only direct rocket strikes will hurt him, and
these yield only 20–160 damage with a direct hit, which, roughly speaking,
means he'll soak up somewhere in the region of fifty rockets before we can
relax. He fires bursts of three rockets at a time, which share the characteristics of our own launcher: a 700 MUS speed, 20–160 damage with a direct
hit, and a 0–128 blast radius. And unlike the Cyberdemon, we *are* subject
to secondary blast damage. All in all, this makes him a tough proposition,
tougher even than the end-of-game boss (I'll talk more about her later on).
The mix of how gameplay-tough and visually impressive the Cyberdemon

was cemented its place in gaming legend. Bosses weren't anything new, of course, and they'd always had scale. The end-of-level monsters in *R-Type* (Irem 1987) didn't leave much screen to maneuver in, and it wasn't like *Wolfenstein 3D* didn't have some fairly memorable bosses itself (Dr. Schwab hurling giant hypodermics was always fun, and we are talking about the game with Hitler's robot exoskeleton). But there was something about the mix of a giant demon that was just so fast and so tough and so dangerous. Twenty years on, the Cyberdemon is still the blueprint for FPS boss battles, the unholy granddaddy of them all.

CHAPTER 10

A "Shot-By-Shot" Analysis of *DOOM*, Part 3

Inferno

Back to the mayhem for the final push. We left our hero rappelling down from suspended Deimos Base to the floors of Hell itself, with a short and bloody stroll through its corridors and halls toward an exit back to normality if we're lucky. Inferno, the third episode of *DOOM* is Sandy Petersen's work throughout, and while The Shores of Hell is characterized by the interplay between his gothic-benzedrine aesthetic and Hall's drive for realism, there's no buffer to hold back the full-on demonic madness this time around. As a result, we get some seriously high-concept level design. Petersen describes the basic difference between his work and Romero's like this:

> Well, naturally, I came from a horror-oriented background, and Romero did not. I remember one day I tried to show him Peter Jackson's zombie movie *Dead Alive* [1992], and he bolted from the room after fifteen minutes, looking queasy. John liked fast-paced constant action, so all his levels were filled with huge supplies of ammo and weapons. In contrast, I like creepy horror buildups—my speciality was making the player know that something ominous was about to happen. (SP)

E3M1 Hell Keep opens with us staring at an eye, buried in a wall of skin and flesh. Only it's not an eye, it's a button, and the wall in front of us isn't a door. In fact, we're at the bottom of a pit, and triggering the button raises us up to the floor level of a flat exterior space (it doesn't drop the walls, which is what I'd always thought until I was hanging about while writing this and an Imp popped up at the rim of the pit and toasted me). The floor is made up of intestines; there are blasted, leafless trees scattered about; and the whole compound is surrounded by a brick wall, behind which red mountains reach up to an equally red sky. Gone is the palette of grays and browns; this is livid and vivid. A castle wall and large gate are the only things to break up the wall. There's a button on either side of the gate, but only one seems to be working. Never mind, we hit the one on the left, and sitting there waiting for us is a Cacodemon. To put this in perspective, this is the start of the episode, so we are armed with precisely one pistol and a handful of bullets, and we've just had two Imps to deal with. At this point, running is not an unreasonable response, and we can dodge past the Cacodemon into a small room that splits into two, with a shotgun on a walkway over a river of blood to the left and a door to the right. The shotgun seems like a good option, only the moment we're on the pathway, it starts sinking into the blood. We run again and find ourselves stuck on the far side of the lake of blood. We can double back along a new path, taking damage as we go, or we can trigger the secret panel in the wall ahead of us, which has no visual indication whatsoever that it is a secret panel (way back in Episode 1, we worked out that slightly different colors to the wall textures was a good indication). This trigger also delivers us back to the Cacodemon, only a little better armed. A little. Perhaps we could just dodge it and head to the door on the right. But this leads into another courtyard full of Imps, and we're still desperately short of ammo. So we take the only other door out of there, to find ourselves in a tunnel with no room to maneuver and three Pinkys heading toward us, which we could always lead back into a space where we can strafe about, except the Imps and Cacodemon have filed into the tunnel behind us, and it's just plain carnage. Assuming we survive this onslaught, we can batter our way through to the final room, which has a bunch of pillars and skulls, like a twisted flower arrangement in some kind of deeply twisted corporate lobby. A whole bunch more Imps make up the welcoming committee, and a Cacodemon is the receptionist.

Hell Keep is not a long level, but that's hardly the point. It forces the player to move, immediately and constantly, and sends out the message that the gloves are off from here on in, so the player can expect a few things. First, it's going to get difficult. Second, there will be no more signposts indicating the right way to go or the correct button to hit (and not to hit);

players should have paid attention in the last two episodes. Third and most important, the occasional tricks and traps in the levels preceding these are nothing compared to what is to come, because now the game will start going out of its way to really mess with you.

The second level, E3M2 Slough of Despair,[1] keeps the exterior location, but rather than obvious rooms (albeit with skyboxes), it presents strangely shaped pitted areas with tall rock enclosures, hiding various beasts and pickups. If it doesn't make a great deal of natural sense, architecturally or logically, it may be because it's the first super-high-concept level of the episode. As the player moves around the level, the automap is filled out, and it becomes clear that the entire thing is shaped like a giant clawed hand (fig. 16). This is, of course, utterly unnecessary, and E3M2 is arguably a weaker level than most of Petersen's others. It doesn't really feel much like you are actually accomplishing anything as you play it, unless you clock what is happening with the map, and that becomes the gimmick that gives the level reason. However, a weak Sandy Petersen level is still pretty good, and it's important to remember that there were no rules for this kind of level design when *DOOM* was being bolted together: this was an exercise in *making* the rules. So alongside the process of mining the potential for the engine as a design tool and then refining these potentials to a razor's edge (arguably Romero's underlying design tactic), the fact that the members of the id team were happy for Petersen to go ahead and push the boat into completely weird and choppy waters should be celebrated.

There's been plenty of talk in recent years about the stagnation of the FPS as a genre (which is only partly true, as I'll come back to in the penultimate chapter of this book), so it's really, really important to see levels such as the Slough of Despair as worthy experiments, questioning whether these kind of metamechanics work. *Wolfenstein 3D* and E1M4 had experimented with swastika-shaped rooms, but E3M2 is on a whole other level, and if it isn't entirely successful, we can see shades of it spilling over into E3M6, which is a very different story. This is regardless of Carmack's take on things.

> The later Hell stuff looks like crap today, and that was a case of designer overreach. It's a problem that has historically plagued the game industry up until only recently, where if people overreach what the platform is really good for, you end up with something that does not age well. It might have a brief bit of novelty value, but you're not going to want to look at it coming back years later. It's really only in the current generation of console games where we have enough horsepower that we can do a credible job of anything a designer can visualize. There's still bet-

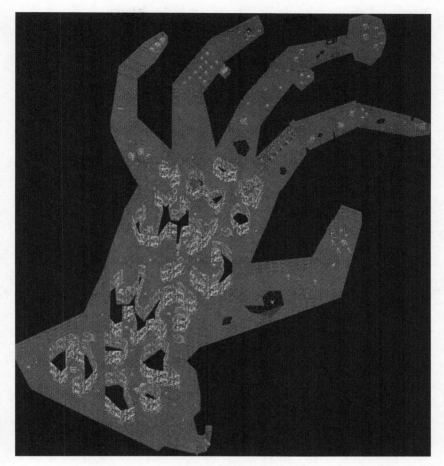

Fig. 16. *DOOM*'s E3M2 Slough of Despair, showing the claw-shaped level design. (From Ian Albert, www.ian-albert.com/doom_maps.)

ter and worse choices, but back in the *DOOM* days, there were clearly things that work well and things that really did not work well. Luckily we had the good fortune that the stuff that worked really well was all front-loaded. If people were hooked on the gameplay, they probably forgave us the later stuff. (JC)

I think Carmack is being harsh here. It's true that Petersen's levels can be eye-watering and are not as tightly successful as Romero's, but from a historical perspective, the experimentation going on in levels like Slough of

Despair has as much of a legacy in FPS level design as that in Episode 1. The move away from constant combat to exploration and conceptual puzzle has been particularly influential, and you might argue that Petersen casts every bit as much of a shadow onto DOOM 3, even if Romero's work has weathered slightly better. It's also important to reiterate how much of DOOM's visual style comes down to Adrian Carmack and Kevin Cloud and that what John Carmack is referring to here is the technical visualization rather than the assets and art direction, which are consistently excellent. As noted earlier too, the color palette of the engine was very much geared toward a limited color run that Romero stuck to in Episode 1 and that Petersen basically threw out of the window. As a result, the environments are *less optimized* for the engine as the game progresses.

The third level, Pandemonium, reintroduces the kind of sprawling, complex environment absent from the first two levels of the episode. Opening into a stony corridor, the level quickly throws a succession of diverse gothic environments at us: a wooden exterior courtyard leads to winding skin passageways, themselves ending in steel chambers or blood pits. Imps lurk in wall cages in front of skull racks. The back half of the level is like a castle. There are scrolling pillars of intestines. Off to one side, a bridge leads over the only blue water in the entire game, only to dump the player around a corner into a burning blood room, with floating fire sculptures and a Cacodemon for company. The blue key card required to exit the level is tucked away at the end of one of the skin passages, which are not immediately apparent. You really have to go looking for it, which technically breaks all the rules about signposting clearly to the player, by which we're all supposed to live. What E3M3 offers instead is a frantic run-and-gun experience, with wide passages where strafing can really be maximized and with a large number of enemies to really test those skills.

E3M3 also introduces the final weapon in DOOM: the BFG9000. Yeah, the readme file for the shareware version might have called it "the prize of the military's arsenal," DOOM II might have wimped out with "Big Fraggin' Gun," and the DOOM movie might have settled for the inexplicable "Bio Force Gun," but us true, die-hard, kick-ass space marines all remember it fondly by its original incarnation, as found in the DOOM Bible:

> BFG 2704 (red). Horrible hallway-scouring weapon. Damages user a bit. Awful recoil. BFG stands for "Big Fucking Gun." Safest use: back to wall, distant target.

Big Fucking Gun. As it is, as it was, as it ever shall be. Actually, the BFG wasn't originally the most powerful weapon in Hall's book. That designation was saved for the Unmaker, a demonic weapon that caused damage in amounts that varied depending on the demon in question (purebloods it hurt plenty, tech-demons less, human-demon crossbreeds not so much). While the Unmaker never made it into *DOOM*,[2] it's tempting to see it as the genesis of *DOOM 3*'s Soul Cube—particularly as id ended up using a fair amount of Hall's Bible material in later games anyway. Equally, if we scroll back to the press demo, the BFG's fire mode is quite different. Every release of the fire button after it is pressed (unlike other weapons, which fire *on* the press) fires off forty red and green plasma shots in very quick succession. The BFG can be dragged around while the weapon is firing, creating a kind of proto-flamethrower effect. The result is a weapon that fills the screen with sprites, slowing the game down, reducing visibility, and, in an infamous but unattributed quote by Romero, making the game look like "Christmas." Clearly a rethink was in order. The redesigned BFG that made the final game was less frame-rate heavy but worked on a slightly esoteric ordnance principal that perhaps compensated for its extraordinary power by making good use of it into something of an art.

When triggered, the BFG fires a single, large plasma ball forward according to the line-of-sight projectile principle of the plasma gun. This projectile moves at 875 MUS, and and its explosion deals 100–800 damage. At the same time, forty tracer rays are calculated along the projectile's flight path but from the player's current location, meaning that even if the player turns, the BFG still works out its secondary fire along this original trajectory, though the point of origin of the tracers moves with the player. The tracer rays fall within a ninety-degree area from this orientation, and each deals an additional 16–128 damage as a hitscan, according to Tony Fabris's BFG FAQ[3] (meaning there is an instant, automatic damage for objects without any chance of evasion). This secondary attack happens a half second after the primary fire, which itself is not instantaneous, occurring nearly a second after the trigger is released. In other words, experienced BFG users factored in three things when using the weapon. First, it required a warm-up, so it was no good in situations where the player could suddenly face problems. Second, once it was fired, you could and probably should move, so letting off a burst could be coordinated with ducking for cover in the point between the primary fire initiating and the secondary fire kicking in. Third, the tracers spread out, getting soaked up by damage-taking objects as they did, meaning that the position of creatures and, by extension, other players made quite a big difference to how effective the weapon was. All in all, the BFG goes some way to backing up the claim in the readme that "using your wits is IMPORTANT. To escape *DOOM*, you need both brains and the killer instinct."

In the meantime, however, we're backing out of E3M3 and heading off toward the fourth level of Inferno, which really encapsulates Petersen's heady mix of high weirdness and design complexity. E3M4 House of Pain is based, according to Petersen, "on the layout of human guts—you can see the lungs and stomach still." It has a pair of traps attached to three switches to confound the unwary (in actuality, one switch opens the next doors, and the crushing traps associated with the switches are automatic, but this threw me the first few times); it has an open combat section in a series of green tunnels that back onto a large visual set piece; and it has a confusing and strange end sequence of tiny cells, monster closets, and twisting corridors. There's a sense that some weird logic is operating and will not easily give up its secrets. This is in keeping with what Petersen describes as his core design principle.

> Always I was trying to make an irrational chaos, like I thought Hell should be. I also wanted the game to feel unfair, like you were being swamped with enemies, so when you won anyway, you'd think you were great. I always wanted the player to think he was smart. (SP)

Certainly, E3M4 lives up to the first two parts of that principle. While the first three levels of Inferno capture the chaotic, slightly messy feel of Hell, something that had fallen together rather than been planned as such, the House of Pain shares with the four levels that follow it a sense of alien logic, which is somehow more rewarding. Hell Keep and the Slough are both too short and too high-concept to really dish out a sense of place, and Pandemonium is a little too fractured to capture something that moves beyond structural design to a game world in the way that Episodes 1 and 2 do. Again it's important to not be seduced by the sequential fallacy (while remembering that if Petersen didn't build the levels in sequence or decide their order, he has remarked that there was a deliberate attempt to create a sense of progression), but for me, it's in this level where Inferno really hits its stride. E3M4 feels almost like a Romero level in terms of the way it shifts gameplay styles but shares with Pandemonium the wide corridors packed with monsters that drive the player toward strafing, hit-and-run action. However, tacked into either end of this are sections that are pure Petersen. There are odd prison-like structures at the level's beginning, with caged Cacodemons and a teleporter into an empty box room. Then there's the final, cramped, room-by-room switch-trigger-keycard sequence followed by a one-on-one battle with each monster in the game, progressively climbing in toughness up to a Baron. Only the level doesn't end with this climactic battle but then bolts on a final room of pillars. If Petersen was after irrationality, it delivers that in spades. The other standout piece of design, although it doesn't actually affect gameplay at all, is the crucifixion room, which is only visible through slit windows from the large green stone corridors where the central action of the level takes place. It's a large area with a blood floor, into which are sunk several wall-like pillars. On each of these, a marine (or, more often, part of a marine) is chained, crucified or suspended. It's perhaps the most explicit of the nightmarish images in *DOOM*: we've had scrolling gut pillars and skull candles and ichor lakes and skull walls. of course, but this is perhaps the one place where Adrian Carmack's fevered imagination really shines out. After all, there is a difference between comic-book beasts and the odd goat-head symbol and a burning torture garden. And you aren't allowed in; you can only see it through a window, which adds to its power. It's a really terrific, unsettling moment.

This brings us to the odd beast that is E3M5 Unholy Cathedral. Remember when we were talking teleporters a little while back? Well, this has them, in spades. The center of the cathedral is built around a set-piece puzzle involving sequential teleporters and is interesting for the hub-and-spoke nature of its design. Perhaps not incidentally, of all *DOOM*'s levels, it's here that we can find the clearest visual precursors to *Quake*.

The player begins the level outside what is very clearly a church of some kind, all brick and wooden doorways, with four choices of entrance. Two open into the same chamber, a semicircular corridor that arcs away deeper into the structure. The right-hand side forces us to run over damaging lava; the left leads to a room full of Imps. Both of these side corridors bring us to new areas: the right to a corridor following the circle round and containing a blue door (eventually leading to the exit); the left to a larger chamber containing Imps, pillars, and an oddly shaped room. Around the back of the cathedral are another series of rooms: one with a group of seemingly randomly placed, irregular walls, a damaging floor, and a teleporter; another with a large group of Pinkys; and a last containing four switches sitting behind crushing ceilings. The central area contains four closed-off rooms, the door of each facing a central open structure containing a teleport pad. More teleporters sit at each corner of this central area, making it impossible to enter or leave it without being teleported away. The premise of the level would seem to be a sequenced run from teleporter to teleporter, clearing the areas as we go, and there is indeed a sequence, with the correct next teleporter in the center pulsing gently and with the reward for getting it right being the opening up of the next closed-off central room, including one containing the yellow key skull.

What's really interesting about Unholy Cathedral, however, is that we don't actually need to get the yellow skull or to trip a single teleporter to complete it. The blue key is found in the crushing pillar room at the top of the map, which is accessible by running around to the left. Then, by retracing our footsteps and following the right-hand path, we can gain access to the exit room, in what is clearly a fairly generous Romero-set 1:30 par time. But the actual level is far bigger and more complicated than that. For example, we need the yellow key card to open a secret door in the central area, and we can only get to it by going through the room with the odd-shaped wall sections. The central sections are opened by following the right sequence of teleporters, but they only give out stashes of ammo and health and bonus (and Cacodemons and Barons). This is a level for completionists, shootists and puzzle junkies, with Petersen clearly understanding that for most *DOOM* players, it's not the destination but the getting there that counts. Speaking of there, just at the exit, there's a highly tempting, much larger door that leads to a room with a single Imp and recessed skull floor. Just off this room is another, smaller chamber holding a BFG. Entering causes a trap to be set off, which closes a wall between the large door and the room with the exit in it. This wall is raised again by using a button in the BFG chamber. The main trap in this area, however, is an audio trip wire: if a single shot is fired, monsters start teleporting in from monster closets in large groups. It is, according to Petersen, a recurring design template.

> The classic case that I used a lot was an empty room with a treasure (like the BFG) on a pillar, highlighted with spotlights. Of course the player knows the moment he touches the weapon all hell will break loose, but that anticipation is part of the fun. It's not just a sudden "Boo! Gotcha!" (SP)

Of course, the really interesting part to all of this is that, like the majority of the Unholy Cathedral, the whole set piece is completely nonessential and operates on the principle that the average *DOOM* player is never going to be able to resist popping a solitary Imp (though a smart one might wonder why there's only one of them in there). In fact, the skull floor just screams out "Trap!" focusing the player's attention on that while delivering the one-two sucker punch of locking the player in from behind and waiting for them to start shooting. One of the things that makes *DOOM* great is the fact that the trick is never repeated. Gotcha indeed.

E3M6 Mount Erebus is completely different from any level that has preceded it. The entire thing takes the form of one giant outside space, an island floating on a sea of blood. Scattered around the map, both on the island and out in the blood, are a number of structures of various sizes. Navigating the level is a case of gradually working through the buildings to get hold of the one key that allows you to exit (or discovering the secret door through to E3M9 Warrens). Petersen has this to say about it:

> Mount Erebus was kind of based on a Town idea, where you'd go from building to building, each with a different problem. (I eventually used this idea to make Downtown in *DOOM II*). I was surprised when it became a kind of popular deathmatch level at work—I suspect because of all the wide-open spaces. (SP)

In fact, if Romero's work in Episode 1 was to establish the blueprint for FPS run-and-gun tunnel crawls, then Mount Erebus could equally claim to be the first case of the type of exterior building-to-building design (fig. 17). This was picked up and really taken to a new level by *Duke Nukem 3D* (3D Realms 1995), setting the groundwork for town/city shooters from *Medal of Honour* (DreamWorks Interactive 1999) to *Crysis 2* (Crytek 2011).

Mount Erebus is arguably Petersen's finest hour, mixing up furious, panicky open-air battles with cramped, intense shoot-outs in the scattered buildings, with some esoteric puzzles that can leave you trapped and searching for the next step. The net result is a level that is characterized by intense bursts of action in a visually impressive (and garish: the animated red/blue walls of static were monitor-crushingly intense), sprawling space that perhaps creates the most definite sense of an environment within the wider world of all levels of Episode 3. After all, it's definitely fair to argue that Inferno is much closer in feel to Episode 4: Thy Flesh Consumed or *DOOM II* in terms of being a collection of loosely themed levels, rather

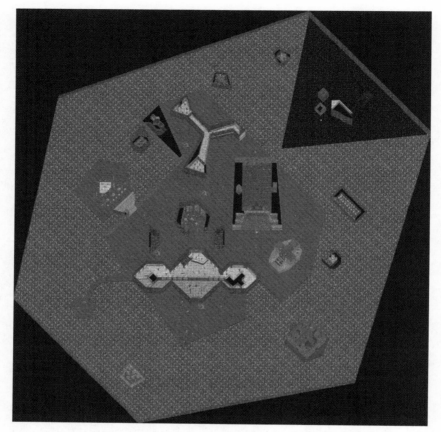

Fig. 17. *DOOM*'s E3M6 Mt Erebus. The arena-style design with small buildings is clearly evident and different to everything that had gone before. (From Ian Albert, www.ian-albert.com/doom_maps.)

than the tightly woven thread of Knee Deep in the Dead, where the sense of Phobos Base as a singular entity is much stronger. As we shall see, creating a holistic, evolving sense of place returned much more strongly in *DOOM* 3, which, even though it ramped up the use of teleporters in later sections, invested heavily in the reality of Mars Base.

The interior sections of Mount Erebus are comparatively tiny (normally only one or two rooms, with a bit of corridor thrown in), and we had experienced open-air levels before (like Slough of Despair). It also hardly presents what could be described as realistic town planning; certainly, compared to

Duke Nukem's downtown Los Angeles, it's a messy and limited affair. However, the fact that it inverts the template of *DOOM*'s design up until this point, where the mainstay of the action is in largely interior spaces with the occasional exterior one, makes it a highly significant, stand-out level. Between the open-air nature of the level, creating a large area for sound bleed, and the fact that entering some buildings triggers monster closets to open outside, ready for when you emerge, it's possible to rack up quite a crowd of fans to follow you around, albeit fans who want to rip your feet off your legs and beat you to death with them. It's the very first nonboss arena in FPS history, and for that alone, it deserves recognition.

We need to take a quick detour around Warrens before we move on. The secret level of Episode 3, accessed through Mount Erebus, is at least as high-concept as the Fortress of Mystery, if even initially stranger. We seem to be back at E1M1 Hell Keep. That button still doesn't work though. Working our way along, it really does seem to just be Hell Keep again. It's entirely possible we may be thinking, "Surely there must be some kind of mistake!" at this point, though by now, the average player is probably smelling a big, fat rat with large fangs and a penchant for human flesh. Petersen strings us along to the very end of the level, right to the exit, before springing his evil plan. Down go the walls, and out pops a Cyberdemon. To be fair, there are a few boxes of rockets kicking about and an invulnerability sphere tucked away at the back, but it's probably fair to say that the Cyberdemon's appearance is a bit of a nasty shock. And it's followed by more nasty shocks. Having dealt with the Cyberdemon, we are now forced to retrace our steps back through the map, and at every step of the way, map walls have vanished, opening up new areas stocked with high-level monsters—Barons, Cacodemons, Spectres, and a whole tunnel of shotgun-wielding Zombies (fig. 18). This final section, like the Fortress of Mystery, is about keeping moving and encouraging the Cacodemons and Zombies to fight one another rather than taking them all on ourselves. Once this last area has been cleared, the mystery switch on the right-hand side of Hell Keep's entrance gates is dropped out of the way to reveal the level exit.

The penultimate level of *DOOM* operates with a mix of wide corridor battles (encouraging a fast, run-and-gun style of play) and a central conceptual puzzle involving teleporters scattered throughout the level. E3M7 Gate to Limbo, like the Unholy Cathedral, has an air of pre-*Quake* to its design and visuals, and in its wall-to-wall red brick and lava is something of a sense of descending further into Hell itself. There are certainly no real in-

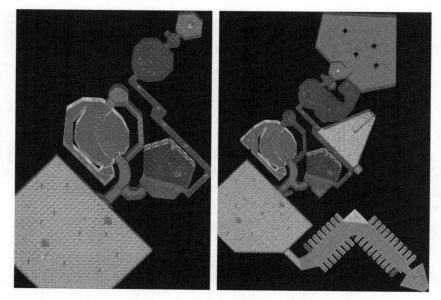

Fig. 18. *DOOM*'s E3M1 Hell Keep (left) and E3M9 Warrens (right), showing the extended secret areas in the bonus level. (From Ian Albert, www.ian-albert.com/doom_maps.)

dications or hangovers from the sci-fi; this is pure gothic. The player enters the level through a number of small antechambers into a large lake of lava (remembering, of course, that every lake in *DOOM* is really just a puddle; fluids on Mars and Hell had supertension that could take the weight of a Cyberdemon, and swimming had to wait for *Quake*). In a tiny island off in the middle is the first of six teleporters (all of which are behind locked red doors for the time being); beyond this is a gap through to another lake with another two island-based teleporters. Off to the right, blue doors prevent access to a maze with damaging blood floors and a large room with a Baron of Hell and another teleporter. To the left, the player enters the main section of the level, a series of open sectors laced with triggering monster closets. The blue key is found in the southern section of this part of the map, enabling access to the blood maze. Radiation suits are found at two points in the maze, but navigating the level is otherwise a case of moving quickly, without being disoriented, to get the red key at the end of the maze. There's a red door by the red key, and behind it is a single switch that opens up every teleporter in the level. The section of map containing the yellow key is only accessible through a teleporter, as are switches opening up the rest of the secrets in the level. Moving between the teleporters brings the player out to a series of rooms connected to each other by windows, containing switches needed to raise platforms and gain access, finally, to the yellow door and the level's exit.

Gate to Limbo is visually more cohesive than some of Petersen's other levels, potentially even tipping over into being rather limited in palette. But the positioning of the level as the penultimate one in the game means that this is perhaps less of a problem than it would be elsewhere. As is, the player knows that they are approaching the conclusion of the game, and it is relatively quick to move about the level, with practically no vertical lifts or drops (apart from going down into the maze area, it's pretty much on a single level) and a central puzzle conceit that is undemanding. Whereas Mount Erebus mixes up an occasionally confusing sprint from structure to structure with cramped and tough corridor shoot-outs, Limbo lets players flex their gameplay skills a little more, accelerating toward the game's climax with a level that is more fun than challenging.

Because, oh, we're here already. We might not have quite managed Radek Pecka's extraordinary forty-minute Nightmare speedrun, but our tour of Hell and its suburbs probably came in at just a handful of hours, in itself one of the reasons why, in a world of sagging, bloated, overextended FPS single-player campaigns, *DOOM* is still a masterpiece. Hello, E3M8. Hello, Dis.

Dis, like the Tower of Babel, is basically an arena shoot-out with a boss, supplemented at higher difficulty levels with Cacodemons. In this case, the boss is the Spiderdemon Mastermind, a large brain welded onto a set of arachnid legs and made bad with a large chaingun. It's certainly bigger than the Cyberdemon, but many players noted that it just seemed, well, less tough, lacking both the visual and audio punch of its predecessor and the integers to back this up. Peterson comes clean about this; it was a cock-up, pure and simple.

> Sometimes I made mistakes—for instance, I thought that the Spiderboss was tougher than the Cyberdemon, so I had the former be the ultimate Episode 3 boss. Oops. It was true if you started the level armed only with a pistol, which is how we always tested, but of course no players ever did it that way. (SP)

Let's put this in perspective, because it's not to say that taking down Big Nasty was a walk in the park. She was fairly tough, with 3,000 hit points; trudged about at 140 MUS; and was capable of putting a fair amount of lead into your average space marine. Her chaingun did 9–15 damage, but in a three-pellet burst for a total of 9–45 damage and at a rate of over 450 shots per minute (or around 7 shots per second). In contrast to the Cyberdemon, this was hitscan damage, so if you were in her line of fire, you were in serious trouble. Unlike the Cyberdemon, who could be tackled with a solid stream of strafing and firing, the best tactic when faced with the Spiderdemon was to loop around behind her, moving each time she tried to turn to face you. Perhaps it was this natural tactical means of defeating her that made her less rewarding as a final boss. If you were good, being able to dodge the Cyberdemon's rockets meant that you could take him on face-to-face. Since the Spiderdemon was using a hitscan attack, it made more sense to get around where you couldn't be targeted. It's hard to feel as heroic shooting someone in the back, even if it is a fifty-foot-tall demonic robot spider.

It's certainly an interesting case study in agent design that the type of targeting used has an effect on player behavior, which, in turn, needs to be factored into the reward system on offer. In terms of the contrast between the two boss fights, the Cyberdemon was certainly tougher, with an extra 1,000 hit points; did more damage on a direct hit; and, critically, had a lower pain threshold (meaning there was less chance of "stunning" it to force a break in its firing for a few tics). It was also a smaller target. This last point is interesting given what we've learned about the strange firing mode of the BFG9000, as it means that a player who can get in close to the Spiderdemon can potentially land on her a large percentage of the secondary fire from the hitscan attacks (given that, at close range and a width of 256 units, a substantial part of the cone of fire will be taken up by her body), dispatching her in just a few shots. All in all, although the Spiderdemon is obviously a tough cookie, the interesting thing is that her weaknesses compound exponentially for the more experienced, skilled player. So this boss is not just intrinsically weaker than the Cyberdemon (although this is clearly true), but the types of tactical combat skills a strong *DOOM* player was likely to use are exactly those most likely to amplify these weaknesses.

In any case, sooner or later, that last missile, cell, bullet, or fist strikes home, and we are rewarded with brain gib on an epic scale, as the metal legs give way, the cortex of all evil goes up in a cloud of beefy chunklets, and we nosedive into the final text. Oh wait. Hang on. There actually is a cut-scene of sorts.

CHAPTER 11

Endgame

Why DOOM *Is a Masterpiece of Game Design*

First, we get the scrolling text out of the way. Apparently, the Spiderdemon was the mastermind behind the whole invasion thing but has "had its ass kicked for all time." Escaping through a hidden doorway, we are magically transported back to Earth, "too tough for Hell to contain," and are left to wonder just what's been going down back home. Ooh, we wonder. Over the dysfunctional chords of "Sweet Little Dead Bunny," we scroll past a cute rabbit on green fields under a sunset, toward a distant city—which is on fire. Then we see the same rabbit's severed head impaled on what's either a stick or an arm (fig. 19), as the words "The End" are peppered with chaingun bullets. OK, granted it's not the most subtle ending in the world, but in keeping with *DOOM*'s overall take on it's story, it's simple, effective, does what it needs to set up a sequel, and, importantly, doesn't take itself seriously (just seriously enough to continue to annoy anyone who's already got a problem with all that guns-and-guts stuff and might have made it through to the end just for research purposes and all that).

So that's it. We're there. We're not finished here, of course. We've still got a bunch of things to talk about. But we've beaten back the forces of Hell and come up bloody and smiling. Now, how on earth (or in Hell) do you summarize a game like *DOOM* in terms of its core design and gameplay principles? What are the overall, underlying lessons we can take from this tour?

First, *DOOM* triumphs because it is the result of a profound and deep integration between technology, art, and design. Gameplay is driven by an immensely well-balanced system of integer manipulation, making it intrin-

Fig. 19. Concluding visual from DOOM. Apparently id Software was not fond of rabbits.

sically rewarding and flexible. Even *DOOM*'s mediocre levels work because the fundamentals of its gameplay are so well balanced and operate so fluidly. The frame rate holds; the game is responsive and clean. The artificial intelligence does what it needs to and doesn't fail by trying to overstep its capabilities. There's a natural, instinctive relationship between available weapons and agents and environmental design. As Romero said, the engine's capabilities drive you toward a certain design. The economy of the tools create a focused, lean, and powerful design space, which is then expertly manipulated to create the final product.

Second, *DOOM* doesn't outstay its welcome. In keeping with the refinement and leanness of the engine, the gameplay is short and punchy. Pretty much all the levels—including the wilder Petersen sprawls—come in at under fifteen minutes, even if you are a slow learner. The whole game is over in a few hours. This means that it's exceptionally tight; there's very little padding or flab. Each level earns its place, and the levels themselves are packed full of set pieces and flowing action that give the impression of being refined and distilled and refined and distilled and, well, sharpened to a razor's edge.

Third (and related to the second point), *DOOM* has a bag full of great ideas and is confident (and short) enough to not have to repeat them endlessly. The sheer number of one-offs in the game (bearing in mind that many of these were entirely novel) is very impressive. This comes back to the relationship between technology and design and to the creation of levels alongside new features being added to the engine.

Fourth (and related to all of the preceding points—you may be able to spot a pattern emerging here), *DOOM* is not built around a "pop star" mechanism. There isn't a centralized, high-profile and singular "neat trick" around which everything revolves. Rather, the game rests on the effectiveness of a handful of simple gameplay tools. You can move, shoot, and trigger switches. There's no physics puzzles, no magic (or technological equivalent), no inventory or resource management. That's obviously not to denigrate games that have a brilliant central mechanic (Valve, in particular, has demonstrated a consistently brilliant ability to anchor games to innovative new mechanics), but the really important thing in those cases is how critical the underlying game flow is.[1] Cloud puts this point succinctly:

> Fundamentally, if in a shooter, running and shooting isn't fun, then you're screwed. You can add anything you want to it, but if that's not fun, you won't have a popular shooter. Every genre has its real strengths, but in a shooter, . . . if running and shooting is not fun, doesn't feel natural, doesn't feel visceral and powerful, then I think you are going to lose out. (KC)

Like *Half-Life*, which also doesn't actually really bring anything groundbreaking to the party in terms of gameplay features or mechanics, *DOOM* works not because of innovative new stuff but because it understands how to wring the absolute max out of the tools available. It's important to remember, after all, that *DOOM*'s many innovations were built around the core gameplay defined by *Wolfenstein 3D* and even *Catacomb 3D,* to an extent. It certainly wasn't built in a vacuum, without precedent. *DOOM* works because it flows superbly, and when it isn't flowing, its staccato bursts create maximum tension-release-tension-release loops that define the template for FPS play from that point onward.

Finally, *DOOM* takes a great concept and then doesn't ruin it by trying to do too much with it. Sure, there's no real story, but there's a great diegesis: a really strong world supports the gameplay and enables a very diverse but robustly linked set of environments to be populated, with an equally diverse set of monsters whose actions make sense to the player. It sets up a clear reason for action but doesn't require the player to get involved or invest in anything deeper, freeing up attention to focus intently on the here and now of play. That's obviously not the only way of handling an FPS, and as I'll talk about in chapter 15, some impressive FPS games since *DOOM* have deviated from this reduced, distilled concept and have succeeded precisely *because* they have done so. But what *DOOM* absolutely nails, in a way from which many contemporary games can still learn, is that unless you are going to invest heavily in all the trimmings of character and plot and ask players to focus part of their attention on these things as well as what's charging down the corridor toward them, spewing molten hell-death from multiple orifices at once, then as far as games go, offering half a story is rarely better than *DOOM*'s minimalist approach.

There are other things going on as well, of course. I've already talked a fair amount about the three major new design features id Tech 1 enabled: sound flooding and sector cut-throughs, variable and dynamic environments (created by designing on the vertical axis and including objects with properties, like nukage and lifts), and dynamic lighting. These are critically important reasons why *DOOM* was so influential and groundbreaking at the time, but for me, the reasons previously outlined go a long way toward explaining why it is still such an exceptional piece of design. We also should factor in the diversity of skills, singularity of vision, and tensions between Romero, Hall, and Petersen, which added to the mix of heady combat, high-concept horror, and visual and gameplay diversity. Particular credit goes to Romero, who selected level orders and stitched the whole thing together. Of course, while I've inevitably focused on the design, none of this is possible without the underlying code or the assets generated to support play, so if there's any sense here that *DOOM* could have been what it was without John Carmack, Adrian Carmack, Cloud, and Prince, that's certainly not the case I'm making.

More than anything else, *DOOM* remains one of those rare things, an exceptionally lean, tight, focused work by an equally lean, tight, focused team of people who all came together at the right place in the right time and threw an inordinate amount of talent at a largely self-generated and gratuitously difficult task. So while we can reason and deconstruct a shopping list of factors that go together to make this unique and extraordinary piece of design, the developer in me can't let the academic in me win that easily, and we do need to recognize that sometimes the magic is in the mix. Above everything else, however, I keep returning over and over again to how tightly woven *DOOM* is, the sheer lack of padding and repetition, the squeezing out of every last possibility from the technology available. At the end of the day, the major reason *DOOM*'s design is exceptional is that it's a profoundly economical game. It understands the constraints it is operating within, and it uses every available means of maximizing what it can within them.

CHAPTER 12

A Handful of Vertebrae and a Headful of Mad

Modding DOOM

Back in 1994, even a diehard Mac fanboy like my older brother had got hooked and was moonlighting on a different platform. I remember him grabbing me one evening after the pub and telling me I wasn't going to believe what he'd just downloaded. Someone out there had gone one better than understanding how inspirational Ridley Scott's movie *Aliens* had been to *DOOM*; they'd gone out there and actually built it in the game engine. *Aliens TC* was my very first mod experience, and it sparked a love affair that's lasted nearly twenty years.

So there I am, me and a motion tracker and a seemingly deserted base. What was so special about the whole experience was that designer Justin Fisher took the bursts of tension that *DOOM* was so great at creating and extended them to a whole environment. The entire first level of *Aliens TC* was devoid of monsters. That just hadn't been done before. It might have broken the arcade rules or assumptions about constant stimulation, but it just shoved the concept of anxiously waiting for it all to kick off to a whole new level. If Frictional Games extended this principle to nearly a whole game, creating probably the most pants-shreddingly scary game of recent years with *Amnesia: The Dark Descent,* you saw it first in the most ambitious, most aggressively imaginative, most obsessive, and (let's not beat about the bush) finest and motliest crew of player-cum-designers the Internet has ever seen: the burgeoning mod community.

Modding is creating new variations on a game by using a combination of new assets, new level designs, and alterations to the game's codebase. Mods can be freely distributed and shared, with developers and publishers understanding that these communities and experiences add significant value and shelf life to their products, introduce new users to their games, uncover new talent, and break new ground in terms of experimentation and optimization. It's no accident that many of today's professional developers cut their teeth in the mod scene one way or another, as did a fair number of the staff employed at id for *DOOM II* and *Quake*. I'm totally biased about the whole mod scene, as I'm a modder. I have been since I got my hands on the DoomEd level editor, since id worked out that harnessing the power of the fan to the dark engine of *DOOM* was an opportunity too good to miss, even if it flew in the face of received wisdom about supporting hackers cracking open your games. Once again, it was the kind of brilliant stroke of business sense that defined the company.

When *Wolfenstein 3D* was released, id quickly noticed that one of the first things to happen was that people started trying to crack the code. There was nothing new in this. Computer science is largely built on reverse engineering and optimizing, and this standing on the shoulders of giants hasn't always rubbed along smoothly with the concept of "owned" data, solutions, and products. While some hackers are undoubtedly criminal thugs just waiting for you to open up that mail about a lottery win so that they can hijack your computer and use it to download four hundred gigabytes of pornography into your boss's iPad, there's also a whole Robin Hood subculture who just can't quite get the concept that people are allowed to "own" ideas or that, because of this, it's somehow wrong to help out fellow programmers by improving their work and letting everyone share the benefits of such improvements. Cue the open-source software movement.

In fact, at the time of *DOOM,* the OSS movement was operating under a different name: free software. The core representative was the Free Software Foundation, formed in 1985. According to the foundation's terms, "free" meant not that you didn't have to pay for it but that it should be freely available. That's a pretty obtuse concept for most of us, and it doesn't take much to misrepresent or misunderstand it. Faced with that problem, in 1998, "free" became "open," and Bruce Perens carved out a set of principles and definitions that still stands today: everyone gets access; everyone can distribute; everyone can adapt and use. You can work from someone else's software to make profit, but you can't use it directly to make profit. The result would be better software and community involvement in improving technology. Everybody would benefit in this brave new world.

Obviously, id Software wasn't about to give its games away for free, but there were aspects of this approach that had very clear benefits if you were prepared to give away a *proportion* of your product. We've already talked about the Apogee model: hooking your target market on the first third of the game for free, then charging them to extend the experience. Enabling users to get access to the build tools so they could further extend their experience beyond the charged levels was equally the kind of approach that a large corporation was likely to see as risky (why let the market have the capacity to build for itself the thing you are trying to sell?), but id grasped, metaphorically, that do-it-yourself stores hadn't put craftsmen out of business. This was partially because, as John Carmack admits, the members of the id Software team weren't actually so different from the vilified hackers that this model purportedly supported, empowered, and encouraged.

> I still today have clear memories of some of my formative computer game times, like on the Apple II with *Wizardry* and *Ultima*. And I would spend time with the sector editor trying to find where the stats are, making maps of everything, figuring out how to do that. And I can remember really clearly wishing that I could read the source code for these things. I remember being able to break into an early *Ultima* and being able to look at the source code—but wishing I could see how the other games were written. And that had stuck with me through the years. And when we were in a position as a successful independent developer and we could go and do whatever the hell we wanted in many ways, . . . going ahead and releasing the file formats and then the source code—those are things I still am quite proud of. (JC)

Call it organizational mentality, but id had already demonstrated an appreciation for the approach that you can't make an omelet without borrowing some eggs off your boss when the office is closed, provided you get them back before morning—when they were liberating computers from SoftDisk[1] to make *Wolfenstein 3D*. Romero certainly argues that id was more inclined to respect the hackers than to see them as the enemy.

> People wanted to make levels with *Wolfenstein 3D* so badly they figured out how to do it, and that was really, really difficult. It was really

hardcore hacking, and when we saw people did that, we thought, wow, people really want our data, we've got to open this up completely. . . . So with *DOOM* we didn't try to protect any of the data. We left it wide open. With *Wolfenstein 3D,* we tightly compressed everything and made it really hard to get at. But with *DOOM,* we left it open, and that just created the entire modding scene. (JR)

In other words, modding was going to happen anyway, so at issue was how best to harness it. You didn't have to give everyone your source code, so you could still sell that through licenses to other companies, but there was no harm in letting a community of fans become raging advocates by enabling them to create and share their own content around the networks. That meant they kept talking about *DOOM* longer; they kept playing longer. You had to buy the full game to get access to mods, so if particularly cool mods, like Fisher's *Aliens TC,* arrived on the scene, casual (shareware) users might well upgrade to the retail version just to try it out. In essence, you took an army of fans and turned a percentage of them into salespeople. Then you could sit back and watch, looking for ideas, talent, opportunities, areas where things could be improved. For the modders, the opportunity to create as well as play was hugely exciting. Tim Willits, who started his id career as a modder, remembers the buzz of creation as central to his drive to mod.

For me, modding games was so neat because it was a world. When I first played the original *DOOM* and when I would look out of the window and see the rest of Phobos out there, I always thought, there's this world to explore—and then to be able to make something that other people could explore and translate that sense of wonder and exploration to somebody else, . . . well, that's still a motivating factor in everything I've done since then. (TW)[2]

In real terms, this is how it worked: packaged up in *DOOM* was the source code, which actually defines how the game works, and then you had WAD files, which defined each individual level. It was these files that players could get at and into, via tools such as the DoomEd level editor, reappropriating game assets (textures, sprites, artificial intelligence, core physics, and so on) to create their own levels. If you wanted, you could go further with other available tools and create new sprites too, which meant rather than Imps and Cacodemons, you could have Facehuggers and Drones, pulse rifles and motion trackers, cargo bay powerloaders, queens and aliens, Batman and *Star Wars* characters, and running around a nightclub pacifying Imps with a spliff. In fact, if you can name it, chances are, in the best spirit of the Internet, someone modded *DOOM* to do it.

We can roughly divide mods up into a few types.[3] On one hand, we have full conversions, where the original game is more or less unrecognizable from the final product (including shifts from first to third person on occasion). In the same class are those mods that achieve a kind of escape velocity and flip over into fully independent games: *Counter-Strike* (Le & Cliffe 1999) started life a bit like this, as did my own *Dear Esther* (thechineseroom 2012). On the other hand, we have mods that stick much more closely to the original game, normally taking the form of new assets and optimizations. Optimization mods, generally speaking, involve manipulating the game to adjust properties of preexisting in-game objects and entities. Often, optimizers concentrate on weapons (which is not altogether surprising, given the genre most mods are still based in), arguing that they create more realistic representations of actual real-world ballistics. In the case of games like *S.T.A.L.K.E.R.*, where level editing is extremely difficult and SDKs (Software Development Kits) are not developed to such a modder-friendly degree, the majority of mods tend to be of this type. Between optimization/customization mods and full conversions are mods that add many new features to the game but are still fundamentally anchored in the original title. A good example of this would be Kalyhanos's *Oblivion Lost* mod (2008) for *S.T.A.L.K.E.R.*, which added blowouts, Burers, and the ability to cook up new superartifacts in anomalies to the original.[4] Finally, we have a plethora of mods that add no new code or assets but create new maps in which play can take place. These are often found around games with a strong focus on multiplayer gameplay—I'll return to deathmatch culture in chapter 13—and it is here that the majority of *DOOM* mods are found. This is primarily because modding levels in *DOOM* is just very easy and, thus, very quickly achieved the critical mass of community skills, tools, and knowledge that has, in a case study from recent years, made Source modding one of the most potent mod scenes out there.

As with trying to reconstruct much of *DOOM*'s history, it's next to impossible to accurately chart either the rate with which new mods hit the scene following release or the total number of mods out there in the world. We can say with confidence that there are still a number of very active *DOOM* modding communities, with new mods still hitting the streets, and we can say that even if we discount the half-finished, the half-baked, and the half-a-line-of-code-got-changed also-rans, we're still looking at literally thousands of substantive, community-generated full conversions and probably tens of thousands of publically accessible levels. We can get an idea of the sheer scale of things by considering the number of WADs that were created or collated for commercial release. Zeta000 on the Doomworld Forums[5] provides a useful list (if largely unverified—I've checked the ones mentioned in the discussion that follows) of commercial DOOM WAD collections, and we can see the volume of levels that made it onto these discs. *D!Zone Gold* (Wizard Works) contained over 3,000 levels; the *Demon Gate Mega Collection* (Laser Magic) a mere 666, *DOOM Heaven for DOOM* (Most Significant Bits) brought another 2,500 to the party. Unconfirmed others from zeta000's list include *DOOM Mania* (525 levels), *The Complete DOOM Accessory Pack* (2,300 levels), *DOOMsday Collection* (1,000 levels), and the 191 levels included in id's own *Master Levels for DOOM II* (1995). Most of these collections have long since faded into obscurity, and many of the included WADs are now distributed around the Internet with the other thousands of freely distributed ones. But this gives us just a glimpse into the volume of mods hitting the streets.

Now consider the expansion of mod culture beyond DOOM. *Little Big Planet* (Media Molecule 2009) may be a cute platformer with a cracking Stephen Fry voice-over, but it's also, fundamentally, a modding engine, a product designed to enable and encourage users to create and share content. According to Media Molecule, there are over a million *Little Big Planet* levels out there. And this is just the tip of the iceberg. *Halo 3* (Bungie 2007) shipped with the Forge engine, actively pushing the idea that it wasn't just about "finishing the fight" but about going Forerunner and actually building your own ringworld. Behind all of these, hidden in a monster closet, are a bunch of Imps and Pinkys. When you play *Little Big Planet,* when you use Forge, when you are working the *Counter-Strike* servers, you have *DOOM* to thank, because that's where it all started.

It's worth looking at a few examples of *DOOM* mods to try and capture the sheer diversity, creativity, violence, and insanity that was swiftly spawned. Alongside Fisher's *Aliens TC,* the first *DOOM* total conversion and therefore the world's first total conversion mod, other existing intellectual properties were quickly reinvented as *DOOM* mods. And, of course, Fisher wasn't the first person to attempt *Aliens* in game format.[6] Back in 1987, Activision gave the world *Aliens: The Computer Game,* which, ironically, featured a first-person dropship flying sequence, and Squaresoft released its own two-dimensional side-scrolling shooter *Aliens: Alien 2* in the same year. The release of the *Alien 3* movie (David Fincher 1992) triggered a wave of movie tie-ins, for Amiga, C64, SEGA Master, and others, again as side-scrolling platform shooters. Interestingly, in the same year as DOOM arrived, SEGA released the arcade-only light gun rail shooter *Alien 3: The Gun*, which is about as close as we get to Fisher (though it doesn't really come close) in terms of capturing the claustrophobic panic and chaos of the movies. Only three years after Fisher's mod, Probe Entertainment brought the franchise to first-person gaming, and it may be argued that not much has really improved since. Fisher wasn't the only mod maker to get the jump on commercial production. Within a couple of years, *Star Wars, Star Trek,* and *Batman* had *DOOM* versions. With the exception of the latter, all had subsequent first-person games released commercially, including *Star Wars: Dark Forces* (LucasArts 1995) and *Star Trek: Voyager—Elite Force* (Raven Software 2000). The plethora of mods being created and distributed massively extended *DOOM*'s shelf life and the sense of community loyalty to the brand, an important factor given the volume of *DOOM* clones that appeared as soon as developers could get them out. Many in the mod community were and still are fiercely noncommercial, and this gives the scene its punk ethos and arguably protects the petri dish of outlaw experimentation we find. However, given that there was clearly money to be made from things that looked like *DOOM*, sounded like *DOOM*, and played like *DOOM*, it's really no surprise that mods started making the leap over into commercial release.

Of course, this was strictly against the rules—mods were allowed on the basis that they were freely distributed and that you could only access them if you owned the licensed game—but that didn't stop products like *D!Zone* from hitting the shelves. The flip side was that if you were into mods in the first place, chances are you were tapped into the community and found it pretty easy to locate and install a vast number of mods without charge direct from the community. But just as with the do-it-yourself store analogy, having the tools and having the talent are quite different things. If the majority of mods were inevitably simple, unfinished, or badly conceived, there were some emerging star modders, and id recognized that players would pay for a guarantee of quality. Following the retail success of *DOOM II* during 1995, id contracted Team TNT and the Casali brothers, picking up the to-be-freely-released *Evilution* mod and commissioning *The Plutonia Ex-*

periment. Evilution was a fully fledged mod about to go public, including levels designed by the Casali brothers, and stands as an early example of the capacity of mod teams to break out of the scene and into full commercial development. This was not, by any means, the holy grail of modders, but an income to do your obsessive hobby wasn't something a fair number of them were about to turn down. It also represented a route into industry for a large number of developers who are now considered leaders in their field. For John Carmack, this is one of *DOOM*'s important legacies.

> That became the standard industry resume, which was a wonderful thing. Mods just became a really truly wonderful way of seeing [talent]. You don't expect someone to produce something that's necessarily commercial level, but if you can see their passion and their willingness to experiment and try different things and you can listen to them talk about what they were doing, what they failed to achieve, what they were hoping for, that was just great. And of course you got lots and lots of people now in the industry who were able to break in that way. And that was a purely good thing—the degree you had didn't matter. It was what you were able to do with a game engine that mattered, and that was the right way to look at it. (JC)

In fact, you could argue it went a little deeper than that. It wasn't just that modders ended up working for id—as did Tim Willits and Matt Hooper, the design team for *DOOM 3*—or even that modding provided a new way into the games industry. Arguably, the creation of the modding scene drove not just the careers of individuals but those of games companies that have gone on to shape the industry itself. Hooper lists companies with high-profile, high-powered staff who cut their teeth in the mod scene: Valve Software, Gearbox, Splash Damage, DICE, 3D Realms, and so on.

> I think if you talk to a lot of people working today on shooters, a lot of them came from the modding community. That's all due to John—I don't think he realizes how much that's true. . . . It was definitely the genesis of the shooter movement. All those guys got their start from the tech John built. All over the place. It's amazing how much. I think some people have lost that fact because it's so long ago, maybe people don't make the connection so much now, but it's undeniable. So many people and so many companies, and it's all down to mods. . . . John laid that foundation. (MH)[7]

But if this drive to create professional standard gaming experiences by Fisher, Team TNT, the Casalis, and other mod stars, such as Dr. Sleep and the Innocent Crew, represented one chunk of the mod community, there was an entirely different and utterly perverse lobby brewing in the blue corner. Over there, the opportunity to go for the comic, the deliberately rubbish, and the just plain barking mad was too much to miss, and the results, gems like *Nuts* and *The Sky May Be,* actually give a great deal of so-called art games a run for their money in terms of inventiveness and opaqueness. *Nuts* features a very big room containing a frame-rate killing 10,617 monsters, where the only way to win is to run as fast as possible over the heads of tightly packed monsters and hope that the lag doesn't catch up with you as several thousand Imps all let fly with their fireballs at the same time. What is fun on a contemporary machine was just plain, well, nuts, back in the early nineties. *The Sky May Be,* a delightfully surreal outing by Doug the Eagle and Kansam, almost perversely preshadows *Portal* or Alex (Demruth) Bruce's *Antichamber* (2012)[8] in its feel. Certainly, it thinks big, overhauling the engine to include some brain-melting alterations to weapons and monsters, primary-color graphics that are arranged in huge and random blocks broken up with an equally random selection of textures from the original game, an invulnerable Great God Imp, and a soundtrack by Bach, with the whole thing wrapped up in a vast 8192×8192×8192 engine-breaking cube. Actually, scratch that, because *The Sky May Be* had its own engine: the Blessed Engine 1.9b Release 2, a self-proclaimed "cure for people bored with *DOOM.*"[9] Troopers move backward and turn into Pinkys when they die. These Pinkys split vertically down the middle when *they* die, shouting "Happy Days!" The BFG is replaced by the Blessing Cannon, which randomly either instantly kills whatever it hits or renders it immortal. Part of the game is set in space. All of it is set in, apparently, the Great God Imp's toy box. There are liberal smatterings of *Monty Python* and samples from *Zardoz* (Boorman 1974): "The gun is GOOD!" If *DOOM* was the gaming equivalent of a particularly dark and frightening amphetamine trip, *The Sky May Be* is pure lysergic acid diethylamide and, according to your tastes, either one of the worst travesties ever committed on a game engine or a bloody mad but bloody fantastic work of unfettered genius. I favor the latter. It's certainly a wonderful antidote to being maxed out on the grim gray seriousness of most contemporary shooters.

The only really sad thing about the whole *DOOM* modding culture is how it tailed off as id pushed further and further technologically. The ge-

Fig. 20. The exterior section of E1M3 Toxin Refinery as imagined by the *Classic DOOM for DOOM 3* team

nius about the original engine was how easy it was to use. Practically anyone with a computer could be up and modding in a relatively short span of time. That didn't mean they would produce anything good, of course, but for many of us, I suspect that wasn't the point. My own meager efforts were ropy, poorly balanced, juddery affairs that don't deserve mentioning in the same breath as any of the mods I've talked about here. I don't think I ever went public with a single one. But it was damn good fun building them and then speedrunning your own creation, however bad you knew in your heart it actually was. Attempting the same with id Tech 4 is a quite different matter, and the torch of mod culture has been passed over to engines like Source and Unreal, which still retain enough simplicity and flexibility to let novices in on the action. Carmack says this was a business decision, that allowing for the mod culture would have been impossible without expanding the company, and that retaining the scale and flexibility (and focus on game, not tool development and support) was id's priority. But that hasn't stopped a diehard community from sticking to their plasma guns and producing modern classics. You can spend a happy few hours reliving *DOOM* in idTech4 courtesy of *Classic DOOM for DOOM 3* (Flaming Sheep Software 2007). You might be able to jump now, and it's a lot darker, but it's still fast and frantic, and there's a fantastic sense of nostalgia in revisiting the Military Base and Toxin Refinery in high-definition video (fig. 20). It makes you realize how much you've missed the place. Thanks, fellas.

CHAPTER 13

Not if I Frag You First

DOOM *Multiplayer*

Shooting Zombies is fun, right? What could be more fun than dancing the chaingun cha-cha with a roomful of the undead? The answer is simple: shooting your boss; standing behind your friends just waiting, patiently, until they turn around, then letting them have a full plasma clip to the head; coming around a corner on full sprint, dodging a rocket, and letting fly with everything you have at point-blank range; taking the final frag when you are down to 23 health and the other fella has a BFG.

As I noted right back in the beginning, the very first FPS game was basically a multiplayer deathmatch. You can find plenty of examples of multiplayer games in the arcades and even via a network such as *MIDI Maze* (Xanth Software F/X 1987), but once again, it was *DOOM*'s speed and intensity that pushed it into completely new territory. If *DOOM* was a groundbreaking single-player game, it can arguably take credit for giving the world the online tournament, the clan, the cyberathlete. The formal structure was there in *Maze War*, an FPS game where you had multiple players playing competitively over a network. And the term *deathmatch* was used way back in 1982 to describe battle in *Triple Action Biplanes* (Mattel 1981) by Russ Haft and Steve Montero, two Mattel Intellivision coders.[1] But *DOOM* added complexity to the proceedings, as well as speed. It had more rules than just two sprites in a simple environment trying to kill each other, because *DOOM* had things like ammo counters and power-ups, exploding barrels, splash damage, acid, and lifts and crushing ceilings. And did I mention how fast it was? OK, well, just to be sure, it was fast.

The description of the game in the *DOOM* Bible is, typically for id Software, a masterpiece of understatement.

> Up to four players can play over a local network, or two players can play by modem or serial link. You can see the other player in the environment, and in certain situations you can switch to their view. This feature, added to the 3-D realism, makes *DOOM* a very powerful cooperative game and its release a landmark event in the software industry. . . .
>
> This is the first game to really exploit the power of LANs and modems to their full potential. In 1993, we fully expect to be the number one cause of decreased productivity in businesses around the world.

The really interesting thing about this statement is that it's not trying to sell the deathmatch experience. Instead, it describes *DOOM* as "a very powerful *cooperative* game" (italics mine). The vision here is not strictly, formally competitive, which is certainly not how the world got to know the final product. *DOOM* was certainly groundbreaking for cooperative play, but it was its competitive modes that really created shock waves. The deathmatch mode in particular, a huge last-man-standing free-for-all, was about to take over the world. Romero puts this down to two factors.

> Well, to me, co-op is one of the most fun ways to play the game. Deathmatch is a more powerful game mode, so people are drawn to it more. In fact, the "attitude" of the game was to kill things, and multiplayer allowed you to kill something other than monsters, plus most people had never killed another person in a high-speed game ever before, so deathmatch was a huge draw. (JR)

Carmack remains somewhat skeptical of deathmatch as a play mode in general but sees its limitations as a result of lack of time to spend on multiplayer and the fact that its late addition meant that the game's scale just wasn't designed for cooperative play.

> The deathmatch gameplay is not the optimal gameplay mode. For one on one, as a duel kind of thing, that's reasonable on there. Co-op, even though we had no design for it on there, was a ton of fun, but the problem was you could play through the entire game in a couple of hours. You'd both start it up and be like "Wow, that was a great two hours, but we're done!" But the other side of things is that there are good funda-

mental reasons why team play is superior to a large free-for-all, because half the people always win, rather than just one person. (JC)

In fact, the really interesting thing is, Bible notwithstanding, multiplayer wasn't that high on the agenda. It didn't actually get worked on until right at the very end of development. "That there was enough time [after building everything else] to go ahead and get multiplayer was fortunate," says Carmack. So the idea that *DOOM* was ever optimized or designed for multiplayer is just plain wrong. Petersen recalls,

> We firmly believed that 99 percent of all players would only ever do single-player. We only put multiplayer into the game because we, personally, liked it. Remember that at this time there were basically no successful multiplayer games unless you count MUDs, and those were penniless. (SP)

As a result, Romero says, multiplayer was never a conscious part of the initial level design and was tweaked retrospectively.

> There was no thought during level design for multiplayer until I was making E1M7. After we started getting multiplayer working, we went through all the levels and started tweaking them for co-op and deathmatch. The network code was being optimized postlaunch, and new versions were included in our patches. The game was originally designed as a single-player game that we added multiplayer to. (JR)

Given that E1M7 was the penultimate level Romero designed, this gives an impression of how late multiplayer functionality was actually added. Having said that, Romero's obsession with deathmatching is well documented (when I spoke to him, he actually used the term *addicted,* a word most game developers tend to avoid like the plague). Petersen attributes the fact that Romero's levels were more multiplayer friendly to their designer's love of the format, while his own focus stayed with single-player, with the result, as he says, that only "some of mine were so suitable." The reason may run slightly deeper than that in design terms, of course, particularly as Romero claims that he wasn't designing for multiplayer either: Romero's single-player levels tended to be built for combat, with the wider corridors and open spaces that transfer well to multiplayer, whereas Petersen was fond of tight, claustrophobic spaces that would inevitably make both cooperative

Fig. 21. DM6 The Dark Zone from *Quake*—a "template" deathmatch map

play and deathmatch less rewarding, as they offer fewer opportunities to work strategically or show off arcade gunplay skills. A notable exception, as we have seen, was E3M6 Mount Erebus. Designing specifically for multiplayer had to wait for *Quake*, where, in the face of Romero's skepticism, Willits placed the first deathmatch-only maps (fig. 21). As Willits describes, once this was established as a model, a standardized design practice quickly emerged.

> If you are making a deathmatch map, and you want to make the greatest deathmatch map ever, follow the formula for all the other greatest deathmatch maps ever and you will succeed. It's really simple. You make a big room in the middle with some elevation changes, then you make a bunch of little passages around the outside, and you're done. (TW)

Regardless of its late addition to the game, multiplayer, particularly deathmatch multiplayer, proved irresistible, even if, according to Willits, its actual impact is often overstated.

The whole multiplayer gaming was cool, but actually not that many people did it, because it was so damn hard to figure out, which is one of the reasons *Quake* changed things more. It was cool to have it in it, and people played on college campuses, but most people couldn't figure it out. (TW)

DOOM offered two multiplayer forms, online and LAN (local area network). LAN gaming was more robust and allowed up to four players at a time, rather than the initial two for online play.[2] LAN essentially meant hardwiring a bunch of computers together using physical cables, which, at the time of *DOOM*'s release, coincided perfectly with the rise of general access computer labs at colleges and universities. We were already camped out in the corners, discreetly mudding and mooing until either dawn broke or the lab staff caught us and threw us out. Was there "decreased productivity"? Hell, yeah. The idea that you could drag your PC around to where your friends had theirs, hook them all up together, and LAN party until your fingers cramped caught on rapidly and has continued to expand to the behemoth gatherings we see today. Anyone of my generation has a LAN story somewhere: my mate Alex remembers duct taping cables across the road to connect up to his friend's place opposite. Who says gaming keeps us shut up indoors when we could be playing out on the street?

Technically speaking (on behalf of the nontechnical readers), this is how online multiplayer works: You need two systems as a minimum. In modern multiplayer, it is more normally three, one of which is a dedicated server that exists purely to manage everybody's game. But you can also use one of the player's systems as a server: they host the game, the other player(s) connect to them, and their computer manages the game for everyone. The conceptual model is that you link together at least two computers running the game (normally called clients) and that somewhere in this network is a server that manages the game. Clients send the server local game information (keys being pressed and computations being carried out, or—if you like, although it's not strictly accurate—where the avatar is, what state it is in, and what it is doing), and the server sends on this information to all clients, to update what they are displaying to each player. So everybody gets a constantly updating picture of the total game world, and everyone is sending local information that can impact on everybody else. When Player A moves into Player B's line of sight, their *xyz* coordinates are sent, via the server, to Player B's client-side software, which renders Player A's avatar on

Player B's screen. When Player B fires a salvo of rockets as a response, the trajectory of this is computed locally and sent to the server, which calculates if Player B has hit the target and passes this information on to Player A's machine. Gibbing follows.

As might be obvious from the preceding description, there are a number of core technical principles required to make online multiplayer work. Primarily, it means you need at least two machines with a stable network connection. If this fails, the game fails. Further, the connection needs to be running at a good enough speed, and this really needs to be fairly equal. If Player B's network connection is slower than Player A's, then Player A can respond to server information faster, meaning Player B may be trying to respond to server events that have, in essence, already passed for Player A. This kind of lag imbalance can be extremely frustrating. Equally, the processing and rendering speed of each player's client-side machine can create an imbalance. If Player A's machine has a weaker graphics card and takes more time to render the server information, this increases the time it may take for Player A to respond. This has a particular effect on more modern shooters that existed before broadband, as hardcore players deliberately set their graphics and sound preferences low, shaving milliseconds off rendering time to speed up their game. In many ways, sacrificing representation for performance flew in the face of the general trends of game evolution, and it's DOOM we have to thank for that. In the gaming world, online multiplay was a primary reason why the Internet just *had* to get faster.

When discussing deathmatch, Romero focuses on the psychology above anything else. He talks of the "psychological issues with out-thinking and patterning other players. You just had a space where you could do much more advanced head-to-head play in than any game that had gone before." Romero highlights the fact that deathmatch wasn't just about arcade skill (the "actual dexterity" on which hardcore single-player *DOOM* play rests) but required a more complex ability to predict, strategize, and adapt at high speed. This expanded the conceptual game space dramatically. For Romero, it is "incredible the depth of psychology that exists (that you never guessed would happen before), even in a simple game like *DOOM*." He recognizes that this expands the core skill set required for expert play: "In a deathmatch situation, there was no precedent for it or the psychology or the strategy you could employ if you were one of the players who could get to that level where you could pattern the other player and use psychology on them to make them lose or reveal themselves." He is in no doubt that "*DOOM* really nailed the psychology of deathmatch."

Let's pause and unpack that idea a little. What exactly do we mean by the psychology of deathmatch? Perhaps a better way to put it would be to recognize that deathmatches are psychologically complex games in a way that single-player games can only aspire to. This comes from two factors: first, the inherent complexity of human beings and their behavioral responses and the innate (and complex) response to both competition and cooperation and, second, the much higher degree to which, as a result of this, multiplayer gameplay is *emergent*. The term *emergent* has quite a specific meaning in relation to game design and game theory. It basically boils down to the idea that even with a simple set of rules, highly complex forms can emerge through their interplay, particularly (though not necessarily) when human agency is introduced into the mix. In *Rules of Play: Game Design Fundamentals,* Katie Salen and Eric Zimmerman are predictably clear and succinct about this, noting that "complex possibilities are the result of a simple set of rules" and that "in games, emergence arises through the interaction of the formal game system and decisions made by players" (2004, 159, 164). In other words, emergence—the generation of complex, highly variable, events that are not necessarily predictable or expected from a basic, often simple rule set—is an intrinsic feature of game systems and is amplified dramatically by the presence of a human agent. This is because human agents are inherently, intrinsically emergent systems themselves.

Game artificial intelligence, in contrast, is inherently, intrinsically less emergent (even though it can be fairly emergent), and this isn't necessarily a failure of agent AI but is arguably an inherent, instrinsic requirement for satisfying gameplay. To put this another way, the bottom line with AI is that it's capable of doing things human players are not, and this has to be kept in check. An example would be AI hitting you with a grenade from a four-mile distance without line of sight because it has the advantage of massive computational speed over a human player. We all know how enormously irritating that can be—I'm looking at you, *Clear Sky* (GSC Game World 2009). So often, the challenge for AI developers is to balance the requirements for the system to be smart, such as in the form of pathfinding, and the requirements for the system to be stupid, in the form of basically letting the player outsmart it. We require *challenging predictability* in single-player game agents by the same token, because it's rewarding as a player to pattern an enemy and beat them as a result. This is clearly a balancing act for designers. *DOOM's* artificial intelligence was comparatively crude—basically just a rehash of the two-dimensional tile-based AI originally created for the earliest *Catacomb* game. That doesn't stop players attributing more complex motives and behaviors, of course. But the reality, as John Carmack recalls, is prosaic.

> It was always amusing when you'd hear people ascribe or anthropomorphize the enemies, talking about how they snuck up on you or cooperated. There was absolutely none of that going on. It was very, very crude and simple AI. They are basically targets that come towards you that you can project some feelings into. (JC)

In multiplayer the focus shifts away from arcade skill, where the patterning is relatively fast and efficient, enabling the focus to be reflected back on ourselves and our own skills, toward a much more complex emergent relationship with the other agents—human agents this time—sharing the game space. The focus now is on their behavior, not ours, to a far greater extent. It's much harder to predict human behavior, particularly when the other agent is trying to predict yours and also potentially trying to give you false information so that your predictions of their behavior are flawed, giving them a tactical advantage, and so on. In other words, if the *Game of Life* (Conway 1970) is emergent, it has nothing on even a simple player-versus-player board or card game, like poker or even snap, where winning is no longer predominantly about skill at play but about skill at patterning the opponent.

So when we talk about deathmatch (and cooperative play, for that matter) being psychologically complex, it's due to a mix of two things. Sharing with other people your emotional response to your actions or another person's actions is inherently more complex. While single-player shooters can, if badly managed, descend into repetitive button mashing, it rarely gets boring either saving a friend's neck or fragging them with extreme prejudice. In deathmatch, every kill counts, in terms of reward. On top of this, when playing competitively, there's not just the penalty of having to reload or respawn; there's public humiliation, which raises the stakes or significance of getting wasted by your grandma on a busy server. Equally, the focus of a multiplayer game changes from mainly skill-based prowess to psychological prowess, the ability to predict and react to a highly emergent flow of events and, if you are really good, to start controlling and manipulating them. It's this that Romero really means when he talks about the psychology of deathmatch, and in both cases, *DOOM*'s speed amplifies the effect dramatically.

The optional rules for *DOOM*'s deathmatch (known as 1.0 and 2.0, the second being released in the v1.2 patch of February 1994) give some indication of the type of action on offer. For example, in the original 1.0 rules, objects did not spawn, and weapons could only be picked up once unless the player died and respawned. This was changed in 2.0 so that all objects respawned after a short period of time (normally thirty seconds). The new rules counted death by misadventure or suicide as a frag against the player guilty of the self-inflicted demise, decreasing the player's frag count by one. In both cases, we can see a change in style of play: away from the strategic "every shot counts" thinking of limited ammo/object 1.0 play toward a constantly firing, even more amped up 2.0 play, with a new focus on self-preservation in terms of using the environment intelligently.

Following *DOOM,* new variations on deathmatching arrived thick and fast. Apogee's 1995 shooter *Rise of the Triad* (featuring Tom Hall on design) introduced the world to capture the flag and rocket jumping, although it was id's own *Quake* that really made that a household term (in gaming households, obviously). The diversification of deathmatch ran alongside the rise of competitive professional gaming, both of which can be read as clear signs that deathmatch, team deathmatch, online cooperative play, and any variation on the basic format of gibbing alongside one another had a very rosy future. It was going to take a while for the fires *DOOM* lit to ignite pro-gaming tournaments and clans—that's for another book—but all the ingredients were right there. Every time you take down a tank in Louisiana's misty swamps, every bullet you take in Blood Gulch, every time your Demoman arcs a grenade over onto an unsuspecting Medic or you ace a bomb run—it all started here.

CHAPTER 14

Fucked in the Dark

Ports, Sequels, and Other Unholy Offspring

Between the release in late 1993 of the original version and the release of *DOOM II* in October 1994, id kept up a steady stream of patches and updates to the game, fixing problems and adding features. Key updates for us are 1.2 (February 1994), which added modem support and the Nightmare difficulty level that was to become a key part of the speedrunning scene; 1.666 (September 1994), which added Deathmatch 2.0 (also changing the shape of the drop-down room in E1M4 from a swastika to a more random pattern, making the game a viable release in Germany);[1] and 1.9 (February 1995), the final version of the game. Also included in 1.666 was Hank Leukart's *DOOM* FAQ, a huge document covering details of modding software that was available and where to get it; walkthroughs and tips for play; multiplayer options; and a poem, written by Hank, called "The Night Before *DOOM*," based on "The Night Before . . ."—oh, you probably get it. It's an amazing document, a huge amount of work, and testament to the fanatical support of *DOOM*'s legion of fans.[2]

DOOM has been ported to a vast number of systems. Ledmeister's exhaustive documentation of comparisons between systems[3] details eleven discrete ports, mainly to consoles: Sony Playstation, Sega Saturn, Nintendo 64, Atari Jaguar, 3DO Panasonic, Super Nintendo Entertainment System, Sega Genesis, Game Boy, Xbox and Xbox 360, and iPhone/iPad. We can also add computer ports: Win95 (an official Windows version was released in 1996, and Microsoft thought very seriously about buying id around this time), Linux, and Mac OSX. These are the official releases; once we add in community-driven ports of the game (including Mike Welsh's extraordinary browser-based Flash port), the number goes through the roof. The majority of official ports occurred after the release of both *DOOM II* and *Ultimate DOOM,* so before we dive into the former in detail, we need to quickly pass over the latter.

DOOM II: Hell on Earth was released on September 30, 1994, a mere nine months after its predecessor hit the Net. As before, the game's story was something of a loose justification of the action rather than anything of any weight, occupying itself with the liberation of Earth from Hell's invading forces. Freed from the episodic model required for shareware distribution, *DOOM II* instead presented a single thread of developing levels, interspersed with text screens, which did preserve something of the episodic feel. Roughly, it goes like this: escape Earth, fight to the gateway, and close it from within Hell. You may want to refer back to the *DOOM* Bible at this point to see how Hall's comment about id completing the arc with the sequel is largely justifiable.[4] Again, levels were roughly themed, although this is far less evident and noticeable here than in the original. Sandy Petersen once again worked design, this time joined by Shawn Green and American McGee (interestingly, Romero is not credited as a designer on *either* game, even though he returned to design six of *DOOM II's* levels). In keeping with the rapid turnaround from *DOOM* to *DOOM II,* there was not a great deal of advance in the engine tech, the differentiations came down to a set of new monsters and the super shotgun, which is still possibly the most rewarding firearm to use in a computer game, ever. The new hellspawn included chaingun Zombies, missile-spewing Mancubi, and two more complex creatures: the Pain Elemental, who fired Lost Souls, and the Arch Vile, who resurrected dead creatures. Both of these added a new strategic dimension to gunfights, and the Arch Vile could be used within level design to steer the player toward particular behaviors in terms of manipulating significance within the environment. It may be relatively simplistic by today's standards, but these incremental steps toward sophisticated player manipulation are the bedrock of modern FPS design.

The game did extraordinarily well in sales, with VGChartz claiming an estimate of 3.61 million units sold[5] and awards for Best Game from *PC World* (1995) and Best Action Game from *Computer Gaming World* (1995). While critics noted that it didn't massively advance the gameplay or tech of *DOOM,* it was nonetheless rapturously applauded. Chris Lombardi of *Computer Gaming World* loved it but felt he needed to point out that "it is not what *DOOM* is to *Wolfenstein 3D*, it is simply more DOOM" (Lombardi 1994). In *PC Gamer,* Gary Whitta hit back at this argument, snarling, "Some may complain that there's not enough new stuff here to excite weary *DOOM* players, that this is just a cynical cash-in, but the kinds of people who say things like that don't know anything. Real *DOOM* purists, in fact anyone who appreciates the game, will lap this up." Whitta summed up by saying, "Like its predecessor, *DOOM II* is sick, twisted, depraved, repellant, morally bankrupt—and utterly, utterly brilliant." His review also noted the subtle but significant design evolution from the original to the sequel.

> The structural design of the new levels makes for a tougher challenge too—the puzzles are more complex, routes more maze-like and things like weapons and secret doors are more difficult to find. Perhaps the most noticeable aspect of *DOOM II*'s new design, however, is the overall mood and tone—it's that much darker and more sinister. Remember those horrible poorly-lit areas in *DOOM* you stumbled into with trepidation, not knowing what could be lurking in the shadows? In *DOOM II* it's like no-one's paid the electric bill in a year, with many sizeable portions of many levels lit just enough for you to find your way around, but not quite enough to feel safe. (Whitta 1994)

Even while working on *Quake,* id was smart enough to milk the satanic cow, and 1995 saw the release of *Final DOOM,* two new self-contained *DOOM II* episodes: *Evilution* and *The Plutonia Experiment.* Finally, *DOOM* was also given a retail release, packaged as *Ultimate DOOM* (April 30, 1995) and containing an additional episode, Thy Flesh Consumed. TFC is generally regarded as by far the most difficult of all the episodes (including *DOOM II*), and the focus on high-octane, supertough combat perhaps reflects the fact that Sandy Petersen went nowhere near it. Instead, design credits go to Romero, McGee, and Green, with E4M7 And Hell Followed designed by modder John "Dr. Sleep" Anderson and E4M5 and E4M9 by Tim Willits, who joined id in March 1995. TFC is a bit sporadic and messy as an episode: this is not a criticism of its levels but, rather, acknowledgment of an inevitable result of the episode being thrown together for added value, rather than as a coherent piece. About it, Romero has commented, "I thought that we should create an extra episode and give the buyers more value, so Episode 4 was born. I had several people creating maps for the episode, which is why the consistency isn't there like Episode 1."[6] According to Willits, even that may be overstating the planning that went into things.

We knocked that out in like a week or two. It was crazy. It was like a week, two's work. Our beta testing back then was just to play it through on all four skill levels, and if you could make it through, then ship it. And a lot of it was fragments of other maps that had never got finished. We were not that clever to have any purpose or organizational skill. Then I think Romero just went through it and saw which ones fell in whichever direction. (TW)

In terms of console ports, there's a general slowdown in gameplay (a perennial complaint about console shooters that gets shooter geeks like me all sneery, *Halo* notwithstanding). Other common features are compromised or missing multiplayer aspects, which is understandable really, given the era of consoles we are talking about; the odd thing like lack of crushing ceilings in PlayStation and Jaguar among others; an increase in bugs (on the Super Nintendo Entertainment System particularly); and, in most cases, a shift to the map order. Sometimes this was due to memory restrictions, as in the case of the Sega 32X port, which contained "a mélange of levels from all three episodes, all lumped into one continuous game" (Young 1994). The really interesting commonality about all of this is how remarkably the tables are turned from the development context that drove id in the first place: console ports tend to be more sluggish and buggy than the PC original. Obviously, more modern ports (e.g., to Xbox) lack fewer features and, interestingly, offer experiences much closer to the original in terms of gameplay and maps. This includes the touchscreen port to Apple products created by John Carmack and the PrBoom team. PrBoom had been running as a source code port for years, following id's release of the *DOOM* source code in 1997. This, in itself, deserves mention, given the huge adrenaline shot it gave to unofficial source ports in the community. The code, when released, only ran on Linux, but it didn't take long to migrate. Team TNT (who gave the world *Evilution* on *Final DOOM*) created *Boom,* a cleaned-up port that then led, in turn, to *Marine's Best Friend,* created by Lee Killough (whose name is familiar from a huge *DOOM* archive now hosted on Romero's own site).[7] PrBoom grew out of these two ports and formed the backbone of Carmack's code work on the iPhone port of *DOOM*. In an undated progress report, he gave his reasons for staying close to port code as it stood.

I am trying to not be very disruptive in the main codebase, because I want it to stay a part of prBoom instead of being another codebase fork. While I can certainly add a bunch of new features fairly quickly, iterating through a lot of user testing and checking for problems across the >100 commercial *DOOM* levels would take a lot longer. There really is value in "classic" in this case, and there would be some degree of negative backlash to almost any "improvements" I made.[8]

Four novels also came out of the world of *DOOM*. In 1995 and 1996, Dafydd ab Hugh and Brad Linaweaver published *Knee-Deep in the Dead, Hell on Earth, Infernal Sky,* and *Endgame,* which take the premise of the game as a starting point before spiraling off into quite a radically different take on events. They were not particularly highly thought of by id, who have always taken a hands-off attitude toward transmedia activities. After *DOOM 3,* there were two novels by the game's writer Matt Costello (*DOOM 3: Worlds on Fire* in 2008 and *DOOM 3: Maelstrom* in 2009), a board game, and a movie tie-in, but discussion of these falls outside the scope of this book.[9] *DOOM 3* however, deserves a more detailed examination.

On June 1, 2000, via one of John Carmack's plan file updates, id announced they were developing a reboot of *DOOM* using the most advanced engine yet thrown at a game.

It wasn't planned to announce this soon, but here it is: We are working on a new *DOOM* game, focusing on the single player game experience, and using brand new technology in almost every aspect of it. That is all we are prepared to say about the game for quite some time, so don't push for interviews. We will talk about it when things are actually built, to avoid giving misleading comments.[10]

Although technically titled as the third game in the franchise, *DOOM 3* is really the spiritual reimagining of *DOOM* for a more contemporary engine. As such, considering how and why it differs from the original and how and why it remains true is perhaps the best groundwork to lay in terms of understanding *DOOM*'s legacy for FPS games in general. Coming in at 785,000 lines of source code (*DOOM* had 54,000),[11] id Tech 4 offered real-time dynamic lighting, which, for geeks like me, was just extraordinary. Essentially, rather than working out light paths and bounces in advance and then dumping sprites into the mix afterward, *DOOM 3*'s monsters would cast shadows as they moved. This is not just a software feat in itself but another instance where a technological advance opens up the potential for some truly extraordinary gameplay and experience design. The most strik-

Fig. 22. An Imp crosses the skylight in Delta Labs in DOOM 3.

ing, memorable moment in *DOOM 3*, for me, is near the beginning of Delta Labs: on entering a lobby area, a huge Imp appears to scuttle across the room in silhouette, a shadow cast by the creature actually running across the glass skylight far above (fig. 22). It's very difficult to convey in print the sense of awe this moment inspires, and the fact that it was all being calculated in real-time, rather than a prerendered animated sequence, remains one of those moments that characterizes for me just how far games have come in a short span of time. Like I said, I'm a geek, and my childhood was taken up with being amazed that if I hit play on a cassette recorder, then I could play *Horace Goes Skiing* (Beam Software 1982) twenty minutes later on the telly. But some things transcend their historical implementation, and the Delta Labs Imp is a really amazing moment regardless of whether you are a child of Clive Sinclair, Bill Gates, or Gabe Newell.

DOOM 3 basically took the central premise of *DOOM* but augmented it with some additional bits and pieces. Cloud describes it as "a desire to maintain the spirit of *DOOM* and revive this gameplay and this universe in a modern time frame" (KC). For example, in *DOOM 3*, we get to be present for the actual invasion itself; the question of UAC's culpability in the disaster is foregrounded, and we get a couple of actual nemesis figures in Malcolm Betruger (English, of course, and with a gammy eye) and Sarge. We have lost the episodic structure, and action remains on Mars Base pretty much throughout, with a quick detour to Hell to pick up the Soul Cube and a conclusion at an alien archeological site, where we close the main portal to Hell. How much all the added shenanigans are actually necessary is questionable really: while *DOOM 3* is a hell of a lot of fun to play, it wasn't ever going to win any awards for deep or complex content, and it does leave you wondering if any of the additions are actually necessary. The original *DOOM* still shows that if things are moving fast enough, story is largely disposable.

The thing about id Tech 4 is that although it was a truly extraordinary piece of technology, it pushed so hard in one direction that something had to give elsewhere. The trade-off for real-time dynamically rendered lighting and the atmosphere this enabled was speed and the number of agents that could be present in any environment at any given time. In real terms, *DOOM 3* is very, very dark, mostly taking place in cramped corridors and lab rooms, and it's certainly much more sparsely populated than its predecessor. In keeping with the direction FPS games had taken since *DOOM*, it does, however, fulfill Hall's original desire to create spaces that felt somehow like the real world. There is no place for Petersenesque splashes of primary color, scrolling headwalls, and vast Bavarian keeps (although the gradual swamping of the base with intestines and gore gives Delta Labs a suitably gross finish). *DOOM 3* does lack a little in terms of immediate visual and environmental diversity, even with some standout set-piece moments, but that's compensated for by a level of detail and subtlety that was never possible in the original. Willits argues that if *DOOM* was a technical feat in 1993, *DOOM 3* was challenging to the point of madness in 2004: "When it started we had no earthly clue how we were going to build [it]" (TW). He describes it as a "paradigm shift" in terms of technology, art, and design. Under those circumstances, compromise in some directions was inevitable.

We've changed from the lean-to-the-point-of-starved "story" of *DOOM* (Fight your way out of Phobos Base. . . . Oh, hang on. Fight your way out of Deimos Base. . . . No, wait. Bear with me. Fight your way out of Hell). Now we're regrouping with our marine squad, trying to upload a call for help, realizing UAC is corporately liable, discovering that (shock, horror) the creepy one-eyed English gimp is actually in league with Satan, being betrayed by

Sarge, and cleaning house by being sent to recover a special artifact that can close the portal. This is all done by following a logical sequence of travel gradually deeper and deeper into the base complex (and thus closer and closer to the epicenter of evil). This requires a convincing and logical flow of travel, a reason to be in each location that joins the dots along a longer arc. The bottom line is that the original *DOOM* just didn't require any of these, because there was basically no linking, running story. So if we went from a warehouse to a castle to the inside of a lung within the same twenty yards, that was fine because it didn't really have to make any sense, and there was certainly very little need for continuity (and as I've mentioned previously, we have to be a little careful about projecting too much of this retrospectively onto the level sequencing). In other words, *DOOM 3,* like other FPS games that use their levels to bridge the beginning to the end, had to evolve its environments more subtly. Furthermore, because it was trying to be "realistic," it had a limited palette of environments from which to choose. This placed pressure on level design in terms of dramatic visual reward, and perhaps the most disappointing part of *DOOM 3* is that any exterior spaces are extremely pressurized runs from one oxygen canister to another, meaning you don't ever really get the same chance to just stop and admire the scale, one of the things that made *DOOM* so special.

Using light as a primary gameplay mechanism was a similarly risky strategy that split players and critics down the middle. Flashlights were, of course, quite well established in the genre by this point. They had the great gameplay value of reducing the player's ability to see and predict what was out there in the dark, and they had given designers and artists a chance to play with a whole new color palette. But id took this idea and pushed it one step further, giving the player a flashlight, but making it a choice to be used *instead* of a gun, rather than as well as one. You can shoot, or you can see. This meant players had to opt for a choice of vulnerability, as Perron notes: "Holding the flashlight enables us to spot the corners but leaves us defenceless, while gripping the gun gives us protection but allows for less or even no time for response" (Perron 2005). Some players had a problem with this, and Glen Murphy's 2004 *Duct Tape* mod quickly appeared to redress the situation.

> Under the crazy presumption that a roll of duct tape has to exist somewhere on the Mars facility, the Duct Tape mod sticks flashlights to your machinegun and shotgun.[12]

While unpopular in some circles (Murphy's site claims eighty thousand downloads in the first twenty-four hours alone), the shoot-or-see choice certainly did change the kind of arcade-skill run-and-gun gameplay of the original.[13] I'm all for anything that induces panic in a player, and it did create one of the most striking set pieces of the game, where a player must follow and protect a lantern-bearing J. Edwards through pitch-black, Imp-infested walkways in Alpha Labs 2. Having said all that, the see-or-shoot mechanism was, as Willits admits, rather less than planned.

> Well, the reason you couldn't attach a flashlight to the gun was that the engine wouldn't run fast enough. I worked so hard to cover that up. "It adds this element of risk, decision making. . . ." And yes, there were gameplay things we did once we found ourselves in that situation, but the genesis of that decision was not we're going to make this crafty experience where you have to switch back and forth; it was we're stuck and now we have to make it work. (TW)

Speaking of infestations, *DOOM 3* trades off population for debris. The original *DOOM* was largely devoid of any furniture, with only a few plinths and the odd barrel to break the rooms up. *DOOM 3* is packed with storage shelves, desks, computer terminals, and other props. Aside from adding a diegetic depth to the world, the gameplay effect of the props means things block the player from moving around, more than anything else. This is occasionally handy, for playing chase-around-the-desk with a Zombie when ammo is low, but more often, it reduces the available space to maneuver in, compounding the already generally smaller environments. Simple features, like handrails in split-level rooms, become obstacles for circle strafing and other classic *DOOM* approaches to combat. As Cloud comments, this drive toward or expectation of realistic environments is not always a good thing.

> Realism is hot, . . . but I don't even know if that's a valuable goal. Believability is though. In an FPS, a person needs to be able to suspend disbelief enough to feel like he is participating in this world. Ultimately it's like cowboys and Indians. A person is, at least in *DOOM*, a hero, and you don't get a chance to do that in the real world very much. So it's trying to get to that point. But believability and realism are two different things, and sometimes I think we go too far in trying to create a realistic environment. . . . [In *DOOM 3*] we were really trying to make environments that satisfied what we felt were the expectations of the modern gamer at the time. (KC)

Of course, it's important to separate out your own playing experience from any claims of objective analysis, but I do find it interesting that Greg Kasavin's *Gamespot* review, for example, argues,

> If you played the original *DOOM* or its sequel back in the mid '90s (or any popular '90s-era shooter, for that matter), you may be shocked by how similarly *DOOM 3* plays to those games. The legions of id Software's true believers will celebrate this straightforwardness as being deliberately "old school," especially since *DOOM 3* is packed with direct references to its classic predecessors. (Kasavin 2004)

Rehak argues that the criticisms of *DOOM 3* stem from a cultural separation "between gameplay and graphics" (Rehak 2007, 151), while arguing that it may be founded in the rise of the *engine* as an entity distinct from the *game,* which id is partly responsible for with the original *DOOM.* In fact, I'd argue that *DOOM 3* plays very differently to its predecessor. It's still a case of run-and-gun, of course, with a straightforward, basically linear design (there's one instance of binary choice in the game, between two pathways). It features a steadily accumulating arsenal and increasing size and power of enemies. But the moment-by-moment action of *DOOM 3* is quite different, if sometimes through an addition of subtle factors.

First, there are normally less monsters in any given space. This is counterbalanced by there often being much less room to move around. It's as hard to avoid one Imp's fireball in a narrow corridor as it is to avoid three in a larger space, after all, but the actual *actions* required to do so (in Romero's terminology, the *arcade skill*) are subtly, but distinctly, not the same. Second, the game tends to alternate between teleporting monsters in around the player as they progress, normally in a corridor, and forcing the player into a dark room where monsters lurk in the many shadows, neither of which are actually that like the experience of playing *DOOM.* For starters, as we've seen, teleporters were actually used relatively infrequently in *DOOM.* The same really goes for monster closets; E1M6 is distinctive for its use of them, for example. Ironically, I'm reminded here of one of Sandy Petersen's comments (although he was not talking about *DOOM 3* at all).

> In *DOOM,* you always had fair warning before monsters popped in to kill you. In later shooters, designers would often just teleport in a monster behind you without warning. Sure such a monster can kill you, but how can you prepare for it? Where is the tension? (SP)

I'm not accusing *DOOM 3* of the kind of lazy teleporter usage Petersen is talking about, although it probably is a little fair to say that the room-by-room gameplay that surrounded the larger set pieces sometimes felt a little formulaic. This is possibly because id had to deliver a game that met the contemporary expectations of game length, which arguably tend to be longer than most FPS games can actually maintain satisfactorily (and it's interesting to note a recent crunch back in single-player campaign length). There certainly *was* warning, in real terms; it's not difficult to predict, as you move through the game, where the next demon is coming from. Because of this and an artificial intelligence system that didn't really feel too much further advanced than the original (certainly given the advances in squad tactics found in FPS games after *Half-Life*), *DOOM 3* did pick up criticism for being too predictable. This is not unreasonable, if it's analyzed as an FPS game in the same mold as *Half-Life, F.E.A.R.: First Encounter Assault Recon* (Monolith Productions 2005), or, well, *DOOM*.

But I'm not sure that's actually the most interesting way of looking at it. *DOOM 3* might not use tank controls or fixed-perspective cameras, but for me, it's right up there with *Condemned: Criminal Origins* (Monolith 2005), *Metro 2033* (4A Games 2010), or *System Shock 2* (Irrational Games 1999) as a first-person survival horror game. Particularly on high difficulty settings, ammo conservation and resource management matter as much as arcade skill. There's no particular strategic or tactical play as such, because, like *Resident Evil* (Capcom 1996), it's a game that wants the player to have to *re-act* constantly, not plan or strategize. In essence, every corridor is an empty room with a pillar highlighted with spotlights, just like Petersen wanted; it's just that there wasn't really that much treasure—unless you count the gorgeous, groundbreaking visuals, which are arguably a reward system all to themselves, particularly set pieces like Enpro's reactor chamber.

In fact, we could push this argument further and claim that the darkness in *DOOM 3* operates along a similar principle as an old-school survival horror game's fixed camera angles, in that one of the most immediate and explicit things it does is reduce the draw distance. If you can't see as far, you can't plan ahead, and every dark corner becomes a potential threat. This changes the player's relationship with the game environment. In a lighter, more open world, like the one presented by *Crysis* (Crytek 2007), for example, the environment is spread out before the player, inviting them to collaborate with the designer, creating a rewarding, challenging gameplay experience that fits their own personal preference. The same can be said for FPS games like *S.T.A.L.K.E.R.: Call of Pripyat* that include many more horror elements in terms of diegesis but float these onto an open-world structure. The world becomes a resource, something that can be adapted and co-opted. In *DOOM 3*, as with survival horror games, the environment is pitted directly against the player, not simply in terms of nukage and vacuums (both of which are rare in the game), but structurally. Hardwired into gameplay is a world that forces the player through in order to complete the experience, rather than offering the capacity to be adapted for tactical advantage. Sure, there are exploding barrels in *DOOM 3* but there is rarely the opportunity to use them the way a *DOOM* player might. They are often in tight, small rooms where the splash damage counteracts the easy kill, and there is often only one or maybe two monsters to try and take out with one hit. Again, this might be a relatively minor deviation from the original game, but I am making an argument of cumulative effect, so it's significant nonetheless. Finally, *DOOM 3 is* relatively slow, even for the modern FPS, and played alongside *DOOM*, you can see where the original's obsession with speed begins to level out in relative importance with other aspects of the final polish.

In the context of FPS games of 2004 and the context of games in the early years of the twenty-first century generally, *DOOM 3* was a technological and visual marvel. Enough praise has been heaped on id for the ground that was broken in its development to last most companies a lifetime. Once again, the sound design in the game is superb. The creature design and animation redefined a generation of what Zombies and hellspawn should look like, while remaining true to the original vision of the early 1990s. If the story is hackneyed and largely forgettable, the Mars Base is stunningly realized and has a wonderful sense of place. It's bloody terrifying in places, consistently tense for the majority of the game, and includes some brilliant set pieces.

And it did really well. Despite simmering complaints about formulaic gameplay, most reviewers were ultimately won over by the game, and it scored consistently highly across the board. It sold too—over three and a half million units, according to Willits in a *Eurogamer* interview (August 5, 2005), although VGChartz puts it at a lower but nonetheless impressive 2.23 million copies.[14] It also spawned a sequel in *Resurrection of Evil* (Nerve Software/id Software 2005). More to the point (at least as far as this book goes), what's interesting is not so much whether or not *DOOM 3* is a good game but how it relates to the original vision: both the intellectual property and the game itself. It's here that we should probably take on board some of Tim Willits's comments from the *Eurogamer* interview already mentioned.

> If you are any self-respecting videogame player, you love *DOOM*, but everyone's vision of *DOOM* and memories they had of playing *DOOM*, and what they thought *DOOM* should be—everyone had a different idea. When you're that popular, you will have different opinions. It was very successful for us, and I love playing it even to this day, and there are few games that look better, still, and that game came out a long time ago.

In line with this, I would argue that the criticisms of *DOOM 3* derive primarily from this attempt to manage expectations of both the original and its extraordinary power to create a notional template for what an FPS game should be. *DOOM 3* may be all about the invasion of Mars by the forces of Hell, and it may be a linear, bridging, accumulative-arsenal, developing-enemy, run-and-gun shooter, just like its granddaddy, but the resemblance stops there. In fact, ironically (given the complaints from some corners about it being derivative), *DOOM 3* did as much to push the structural template of FPS gameplay toward survival horror as the more frequently cited *System Shock 2*. The advances in technology, particularly graphics, were outstanding. But it may just be remembered as quietly deviant in its gameplay too. Which nicely brings us to the question of this powerful template for FPS games, this idea of *DOOM* as the prototypical shooter.

CHAPTER 15

You Gibbed It Here First

DOOM *as the Prototypical FPS Game*

We've already seen that *DOOM* came off the back of a history of first-person gaming that stretches right back to the inception of games as a medium. We can also see the emerging form of the title in the development of the technology and the "prototype" id games of *Catacomb 3D, Hovertank 3D,* and *Wolfenstein 3D.* On the flip side of release, the sheer quantity of clones and the long history of FPS games that follow clearly suggest *DOOM's* importance. Worth doing at this point, however, is siting it more specifically within the genre and seeing how *DOOM* sits relative to how FPS games have developed in the two decades since its release. To open that up, it's worth quoting Matt Hooper again.

> You know, a lot of things at id . . . they just evolve. There's not this Bible saying this is the game we're going to make that's written. It's really just all these individuals and their creative input. . . . Nowadays there's so many production methodologies and everything is so structured, and sometimes I'm not so sure that's always a win. Back then, it was just a really tiny company with a bunch of very creative people who knew exactly what they were doing. So the magic was more than saying, "Hey, we're going to do this"—and to be honest, the tech drove a lot of the direction. (MH)

What I love about this statement is that though Hooper is talking about *DOOM 3,* his comments are more or less indistinguishable from the way

Petersen and Romero talk about *DOOM*. So when Hooper says that, like *DOOM*, the reboot was driven predominantly by Carmack's tech but also "wanted to stay true to the shooter roots," that begs the question of whether this way of doing things is limited to id, whether this idea of "shooter roots" is one studio talking, or whether *DOOM* is woven into the fabric of a wider group of games.

Bateman and Boon (2006), in their discussion of genres, talk about the idea of a "nucleating game," a prototypical template or even a kind of "pure form." *DOOM* is an obvious candidate for the pure form of FPS, and examining it together with how other titles deviate from this template can tell us some interesting things about the wider genre as well as reflect this understanding back onto *DOOM* itself. It may, for example, help us to understand if the ongoing classic status of the game rests on more than simply nostalgia. To do this, we should return to the basic mechanics of the game, specifically the relationship between code, player, and system.

One way we can understand this relationship is to look at what it is a game actually lets a player do. These are sometimes called affordances, that is, what the system "affords" the player the capacity to do.[1] The modern concept of affordances should be credited to the psychologist J. J. Gibson (1979), as an alternate way of understanding how we deal with the world and the objects we encounter in it. Rather than seeing our navigation and understanding of our surrounding environments as being based on the perception of physical properties, such as mass or color, Gibson argued that this perception is more likely to focus on affordances. In other words, our perception is based around function, rather than form. So when we see an Xbox, we're thinking not "It's a grayish box with a few buttons on the front, around thirty centimeters high and fifteen centimeters wide, and looks like it weighs a couple of kilos" but, rather, "Ooh! Halo!"

Alternatively, think about a chair. Gibson's argument was that although we can use chairs for many things, we use them primarily for sitting on, and this dominant affordance is what we perceive first and foremost when we see a chair. This flips back around in the other direction too: we could argue that we determine an object is a chair because we identify its dominant affordance as enabling us to sit on it. This two-way process is really very useful when we start to think about games and gameplay mechanics. Breaking media down into constituent parts isn't fashionable in game studies right now, but the advantage of taking what's really a kind of structuralist approach is that it helps build up a body of baseline data that we can use to compare titles within a genre. It also helps us get a better understanding of how, for instance, diegetic and ludic elements relate to one another (particularly when they exist in the same object), because it means we can understand game content as a functional device—a provider of affordances, if you like—in the way I alluded to at the beginning of chapter 9. You can push this to a formal extreme, taxonimizing objects according to the types of affordances they exhibit (Pinchbeck 2009a), which can be a powerful analytical method, as it enables us to fill in the normal blanks between rule sets and their implementation as (diegetic/ludic) mechanics, something game studies has singularly failed to achieve.

This structuralist approach allows us to illustrate a genre by getting beyond the normal interpretative reading (attained by hunting for the meaning in game objects) through doing something that's actually quite a lot simpler. By literally "counting barrels in *Quake 4*" (Pinchbeck 2007), we find out how many barrels there are and how they are used. This might seem a little banal, but if we compare the numbers and placements of barrels in *Quake 4* and a whole bunch of other games, we end up getting told something about *Quake 4* and that other bunch in the process. If it sounds simplistic, well, it is. But the lack of this baseline data gathering in game studies is frankly astonishing and leaves the field with huge vacuums of knowledge that can only be filled by interpretation, theory and, at worst, guesswork. The structuralist approach may not be able to tell us everything—far from it—or turn out to be that accurate or even useful in the long run, but following the process generates the raw data we need to compare games across a genre. That's the only way we are going to be able to answer questions like "Is *DOOM* a prototypical—or even typical—FPS game?" We need to sit back and count the affordances, to see what the actual structure of gameplay (both ludic and diegetic and that horribly messy way they interrelate and coexist) is like from the inside.[2]

In *DOOM*'s case, we have free movement along a horizontal axis—forward, backward, and left/right at ninety degrees of the way the avatar is facing (using an additional key input or dedicated strafing keys). On top of this, we have key bindings for generic interaction (to open door, press button), attacking (one key for melee and shooting), and sprinting; shortcuts for choosing weapons; a map function; and main menu options for loading, saving, and so on. A mouse can be enabled to take on shooting, strafing, and moving forward, as well as taking over orientation as a free look function. *DOOM* has no vertical controls—no jump, no looking up or down. It does have split-level environments, but objects at a different height to the player are automatically targeted.

After *Quake* expanded these basic affordances with jumping and crouching, as well as offering vertical orientation and aiming, these extensions were subsequently adopted by the overwhelming majority of FPS games. Rollings and Adams agree that "the *DOOM* and *Quake* modes of interaction for FPS games are pretty much ubiquitous nowadays" (Rollings and Adams 2003, 313),[3] and it is rare to find games that deviate from this basic template. *Condemned: Criminal Origins* and *Painkiller* (People Can Fly 2005) are notable by their lack of crouch functions. Sprinting is less ubiquitous, often replaced with a walk/sneak alternative, and even fewer games allow a "peek around corners" through a special key binding. By analyzing key bindings, we instantly begin to get clues as to the type of gameplay on offer. Allowing an action usually means that the action is designed for use in the game. Allowing players to sneak suggests to them fairly explicitly that it is, at least on occasion, advantageous to do so. It is also interesting that these types of functionality are not simply products of FPS games evolving in terms of their technical capabilities; they prompt and enable exactly the type of gameplay id made a conscious decision to *remove* from *Wolfenstein 3D*. At the root of this is an obvious logic: the presence of more affordances means more complex gameplay, in the form of more potential buttons to press and more potential configurations of action. In contemporary FPS games, simplicity in what we could call exploratory affordances (jump, crouch, sprint, sneak, peek) are found in games such as *Painkiller, Resistance: Fall of Man* (Insomniac 2007), *Quake 4, Unreal Tournament* (Epic Games/Digital Extremes 1999), *Prey,* and the *Halo* franchise. Even with the most cursory of glances, complex exploratory affordance games like *S.T.A.L.K.E.R.* or *Thief: Deadly Shadows* (Ion Storm 2004) clearly belong in a different class. In terms of prototypes, they have deviated from *DOOM*'s template in terms of what exploratory actions of gameplay are possible, by adding more key bindings, more things to do; and the gameplay shifts accordingly.

We can apply a similar process to how we look at combat. *DOOM* offers no alternate fire modes for its weapons, allows players to carry all their available weapons at once, does not develop or evolve any carried weapons during the game, and does not force players to reload—ammunition is simply fired until the weapon is empty. All of these factors create a model for gameplay best understood by examining the alternatives. A zoom or scope creates a heightened strategic dimension to combat (like the crouch function), suggesting that location and vantage are now major tactical advantages. Alt-fires create a similar strategic dimension. They change the player's relationship with the environment. *DOOM*'s players, like *DOOM 3*'s, are placed in a fundamentally *reactive* relationship with the environment. *Far Cry* or *Half-Life 2*'s players operate *proactively*. Limiting the number of weapons available at any given time, whether this is fixed (as in *Halo* or *Crysis*) or managed by inventory or weight (as in *S.T.A.L.K.E.R.* or *System Shock 2*) forces the player to think about their avatar's capabilities, relative to their skills and preferences and the potential situation they are heading into. It slows play down. Similarly, a fixed magazine capacity for weapons means that players need to consider an additional factor in combat, as reloading inevitably disadvantages them. The lack of these strategic elements reaffirms Romero's argument that *Wolfenstein 3D* and, by extension, *DOOM* were arcade games first and foremost.

> The goal was to remove anything like stealth, because for me as a designer and a player, when I have things I can hide behind, crouch, or sit there taking damage like a bullet sponge, that's not skill. That's not a skillful way to play a game. I came from the arcades, and that's all about speed. (JR)

So the lack of any form of configurative activity, strategic planning, or asset management on the part of the player really defines the type of game *DOOM* is. Interestingly, in *DOOM,* we see the core affordances laid down for the genre (or reaffirmed really, as the template was essentially there from *Maze War*), but in terms of the experience of gameplay, all of these small incremental nods to strategy and planning mean that the vast majority of contemporary FPS games deviate from *DOOM*'s flavor in subtle but significant ways.

Despite *DOOM*'s position as the mother lode of first-person shooters, when we consider the impact of these additional affordances as having the effect of making play slower and more complex, the spirit of *Ultima Underworld: The Stygian Abyss* rears its head once more. Both *System Shock* (Looking Glass Studios 1994) and its sequel, for example, certainly make extensive use of *DOOM*'s dark-edge horror imagery and some technical tricks, such as leaking audio being used to manipulate mood in exploratory phases before combat kicks off. But in many other ways, these are games of configuration, where making smart choices outside the pressure of real-time gameplay have as much impact on success as any second-by-second skill (not that this is entirely lacking, of course, as anyone who has run out of ammo halfway through a Rumbler charge will attest to).

Having said that, the blunt fact is that although it might not be the defining feature of the genre, the vast majority of FPS games are built around blowing a range of demons, aliens, cyborgs, reanimated corpses, communists, Nazis, North Koreans, or Africans—or whatever culture is currently permissible as a target for the marketplace—into bloody chunks. This returns us to Cloud's take on things: "Fundamentally, if in a shooter, running and shooting isn't fun, then you're screwed" (KC). However, we can remove from the equation the diegetic elements (the actual representations chosen by the developers) and talk about what is expected in FPS games in purely structural, ludic terms. Most games are actually about configurative activity, in reality. You are presented with a form of pattern, whether this is infinitely repeating, as in *Tetris* (Alexey Pazhitnov 1984), or moving toward a final ending, as in *Gears of War* (Epic Games 2006). This pattern is made up of objects in an environment, some of which you can manipulate in certain ways. By manipulating the right objects in the right way, in the right order, at the right time, you get an outcome. In other words, you adjust the pattern until it fits an acceptable range of configurations.

In an FPS game, the underlying pattern manipulation is usually very simple. You are presented with an environment with lots of objects in it. Gradually, you reduce this complexity to its simplest form by removing agents, triggering switches, and using ammo packs and health kits. Then you move on to another complex environment and do the same thing, until the world is saved, the Nihilanth is a headless lump, Hitler's giant fighting exoskeleton is a pile of twisted metal, or whatever the ultimate goal is. This is primarily achieved by lining up objects with the vanishing point (the center of the screen) and removing them. There are other things also: buttons to press, lifts to call, missiles to launch, and hostages to rescue. But it's the same basic pattern: a limited range of affordances applied to a limited range of objects and a pretty basic process of configuration in order to progress. So what we are really talking about here, in terms of *DOOM's* prototypical position in the FPS genre, is how much additional complexity we're bolting on in terms of configurative affordances. At some point, we need to make a decision and ask whether a game like *Fallout 3*, which combines first-person perspective with an extremely high emphasis on configurative affordances, should be classified as an RPG with first-person perspective and whether *Ultima* is really a qualitatively different game to *DOOM*. Clearly, this should give us pause to consider why we require such classifications in the first place. In this case, for example, we could play devil's advocate and argue that *Fallout 3* doesn't have *DOOM* as a prototype in its lineage, as it's a configuration-centered RPG that utilizes first-person perspective, derived directly from *Ultima Underworld,* which relegates the entire FPS genre to an interesting parallel. To understand *DOOM*'s legacy, therefore, we need to consider a number of ways in which the genre has developed, so we can trace influence and impact in more detail.

We have a genre of games with a reduced but direct perceptual mapping between avatar and player, where the defining structural characteristic is the simplification of the environment. This structure is bolted on top of a relatively small set of affordance relationships between an equally small set of basic object classes, most of which have predetermined affordance relationships built into them. And there's our FPS. Expanding from the purely structural, we can normally expect from an FPS the following conditions or scenarios:

A central avatar figure that the player is expected to strongly identify with (particularly given that they see the world through this (first) person's perspective)

A dangerous or unknown environment to be navigated

A selection of aggressive agents to be removed from the environment as the core short-term act of play

A (more or less) linear story presenting a conflict to be resolved by the player

The ability to move, look, jump, run, crouch/sneak, and shoot

Multiple means of removing agents from the environment

Taking all of that on board, we can trace a pretty direct line from *DOOM* to more modern incarnations of this centralized format: *Half-Life, Halo,* the *Resistance* and *Killzone* franchises, *Wolfenstein, F.E.A.R., Painkiller, Crysis, Prey, Far Cry 2, Quake 4, Singularity* (Raven Software 2010), and *Bulletstorm.* In all of these games, we find a linear progression through a dangerous environment by a lone protagonist, with an increasing diversity of agents balanced by an increasing arsenal of weaponry. However, even in this list, we can find examples of how the genre has diversified in terms of added features.

For example, *Halo* presents an alternative to free selection of a large number of weapons, instead allowing the player access to only two at any given time. This model is followed by the *Far Cry* and *Crysis* games and elsewhere by *Left 4 Dead* and *Left for Dead 2* (Valve Software 2008, 2009). The replacement of free selection with limited access creates an alternate strategic dimension to play, replacing very clear signaling to the player of progression toward the end of the game, likely strength of agents, and suggested tactical approach to the forthcoming situation (the bigger the available guns, the bigger the approaching horde) with an open approach to strategy and player-selected tactics. Another diversification we can note is the increase of sandbox-type levels, where the player has greater scope for approaching the environment in a personalized manner, typified by *Crysis* and seen elsewhere in *S.T.A.L.K.E.R.: Shadow of Chernobyl* and, to a lesser extent, *Halo*. Sandbox environments bring these prototypical linear shooters closer to a multiplayer model by using arena-style areas: these are found in *Crysis, Far Cry 2, Painkiller,* and *Resistance* and offer a gameplay style that is found more commonly in the multiplayer shooters *Unreal Tournament, Left 4 Dead,* and *Enemy Territory: Quake Wars* (Splash Damage 2007).

The capacity to play over a LAN and, later, the Internet has been core to the genre since DOOM, and we should really consider multiplayer capability as a feature of prototypical FPS games. However, starting with *Quake III: Arena* (id Software 1999), we can begin to note a shift in emphasis in some games from multiplayer as a supplement to single-player to the opposite. The *Unreal Tournament* series, for example, consists principally of multiplayer games designed for online competitive and cooperative play, with short, perfunctory single-player campaigns bolted somewhat halfheartedly on top. *Enemy Territory, Counter-Strike, Red Orchestra* (Tripwire Interactive 2006), *Left 4 Dead,* and *Starsiege: Tribes* (Dynamix 1998) are all about multiplayer capacity, and we can see the shift in emphasis in single-player titles such as *Halo 3* and *Call of Duty: Modern Warfare 2,* whose very short single-player campaigns simply do not carry the weight of the multiplayer possibilities. So we can posit an axis of divergence from the prototype (which has multiplayer capability and even optimization), through predominantly single-player titles with multiplayer capacity (the majority of the genre) and predominantly multiplayer titles with single-player capacity (e.g., *Modern Warfare 2*), to multiplayer-only FPS games (e.g., *Left 4 Dead* and *Counter-Strike*).[4]

Less prototypically, there are RPG crossovers. In reality, this means that a significant degree of configuration of the avatar is allowed. This may be limited to inventory (which, as previously noted, we can view as really an extension or set of mediating parameters through which the player's affordances are managed in the world), as we find in *Bioshock*, *S.T.A.L.K.E.R.*, *No One Lives Forever* (Monolith 2000), and *Perfect Dark Zero* (Rare 2005). This then extends into configuration of the avatar itself at the start of play, as in *System Shock 2*, where the player can choose character classes that have an important impact on the skills that can be used (a major affordance adjustment). The idea of separated skills and abilities, as also found in *Deus Ex*, begin to move the games into the populist genre classification of the RPG, with a downgraded emphasis on combat and an increased focus on avatar development, classically through leveling-up skills. *Fallout 3*, *The Elder Scrolls IV: Oblivion* (Bethesda 2006), and *Hellgate: London* (Flagship Studios 2007) are all examples of role-playing games with a strong FPS element to them.

Lastly, a significant deviation from the prototype sees some games downplay the central combat element of the genre in favor of puzzles or exploration. Most famously, *Portal* and *Mirror's Edge* both eschew combat almost completely, replacing it with physics-based problem solving in the former and sequence-driven movement in the latter. *Call of Cthulhu: Dark Corners of the Earth* (Headfirst Productions 2006) really belongs on this outer spiral too, with its heavy focus on story, slow placing, and extremely dangerous and unwelcome combat. For the same reasons, the deliciously weird, if flawed, *Pathologic* (Icepick Lodge 2005) is cut from the same cloth as both *Cthulhu* and the puzzle-orientated *Penumbra* series (Frictional Games 2007, 2008). We can also suggest that the *Condemned* series, as a core example of FPS gaming with a focus on melee rather than distance attacks, belongs in this group, as does *Dark Messiah of Might and Magic* (Arkane Studios 2006), for the same reason.

The preceding discussion identifies five potential axes of movement from the prototypical shooter: emphasis on strategy, sandboxing, multiplay, high configuration (RPG), and non-combat orientation. I am not claiming this is a final means of illustrating the genre, but it does at least offer a better system than the normal dialectic boundary-making exercises we sometimes find in game studies. Arguably, *DOOM* represents the first significant move from purely reactive arcade play, by increasing the complexity of environments, breaking up ammo into weapon types, having a range of albeit simple weapon behaviors (and agent behaviors), and, crucially, making environmental exploration its own reward. In levels like Mount Erebus and the final boss battles, we have very early arena-style environments, which may eventually lead to sandboxes. More to the point, the creation of the multiplayer scene may also factor into this, and *DOOM* certainly can take some credit for that. Configuration, of course, was something id's games actively rejected. Todd Hollenshead argues that regardless of any of these evolutions, the core game at the center of even the most left-field FPS has a clear origin.

> Nolan Bushnell is quoted as saying *Halo* is the same as *DOOM* with better graphics. He meant that as an insult to *Halo,* but I actually take it as a compliment. And I think, in many ways, it is absolutely true. All shooters still follow the same fundamental game mechanic that id created with *Wolfenstein 3D* and *DOOM.* We can just do a much more sophisticated and graphically rich job of execution of that formula today. (THo)

The other direction in which contemporary shooters have moved away from *DOOM* is the increasing sense of importance given to complex story and world. We have FPS games being used to underpin extended essays on utopia and free will (*Bioshock*), the futility of war and loss of innocence (*Far Cry 2*), antiglobalism and civic dissent (*Mirror's Edge*). We have attempts to realistically portray warfare in all its chaos (*Modern Warfare 2, Arma 2* [Bohemia Interactive 2009]). We have worlds that draw inspiration from avant-garde Soviet sci-fi novels and films (*S.T.A.L.K.E.R., Pathologic, Metro 2033*). On top of all these commercial developments, we have a fan culture comprised of thousands of modders creating, adapting, sharing, experimenting, pushing at the boundaries of what this genre is and can do. This runs contrary to the argument that traditional FPS games do little more than fetishize violence, weaponry, and aggression; that they often center around a right-wing libertarian political stance; and that they are predominantly male power fantasies. For example, Bittanti (2006) argues, "The FPS can be read as a stylized sex-hunting game—the always-erect gun looks for virtual bodies so that he can impregnate them with bullets—there is no other way of negotiating the encounters with other characters."

While I find these kinds of readings of games highly dubious, titles such as *Modern Warfare 2* do seem to go out of their way to conform to the idea of a libertarian power fantasy. Efforts to do so range from offering opportunity to extract righteous vengeance of a wronged and invaded United States; to explicitly connecting gamer satisfaction with a parade of high-tech military technology, from sidearms to remote-controlled killer drones; right down to quoting Dick Cheney in loading screens. We should also remember *America's Army* (U.S. Army 2002), which was explicitly developed as a recruitment tool for the real America's army (Nieborg 2004). This aside, most FPS games, like *Modern Warfare 2,* are careful to position the avatar in a reactive role:[5] the crusader who is fighting either for his or her life (*Half-Life*), loved ones (*Prey*), or the greater causes of freedom, humanity and/or right (*Deus Ex, Resistance, Quake 4*).

In fact, we can argue that alongside the economic reality developers work within (in other words, what is likely to drive sales), one of the reasons that we find the content of FPS games we do is that it marries particularly well to the ludic structures that have evolved within the genre. For example, isolation, a common theme in FPS games, takes its roots in the processing capabilities of early platforms. In *DOOM,* for example, the artificial intelligence is simply not advanced enough to cope with multiple friendlies—it's really *Halo,* seven years later, where this first starts appearing properly (advances in AI such as in *Half-Life* and *Quake III: Arena* notwithstanding). Story and gameplay, when well designed, operate seamlessly and interweave with one another, and so it's no surprise that the early shooters offer many variations on the basic theme of being adrift and individually responsible for resolving whatever crisis is presented. For example, *DOOM's* marine is literally the last survivor, left behind to guard the shuttle; *System Shock's* hacker awakes from a coma to find that a disaster has already happened; the cyborg supersoldier in *Marathon* (Bungie 1994) is set apart from the rest of the population. These recurring justifications for a lone avatar remain central to FPS stories, right up to id's 2011 release *Rage,* and thus inform any political reading of the games.

However, as technologies have enabled more complex experiences to be leveraged into the basic FPS structure, this lone-wolf libertarianism has been supplemented by non-player characters (NPCs) and squad mates. Bot squad mates were really an inevitable response to the popularity of online multiplayer FPS games—itself arguably created by *DOOM's* deathmatch culture. NPCs are a powerful means of deepening the experience emotionally by offering engaging humanized representations of themes, issues, and symbols. More important, they are exceptionally powerful ludic objects. NPCs are particularly useful as signposting devices, offering players' orientation information as well as direct links to goals and targets. They also enable the occurrence in the game world of complex actions outside the limited affordance set available to the player—hacking computers, handling communications and tactics, and so on (Pinchbeck 2009b).

What is interesting about NPCs used in this way is that they are frequently not represented visually. *Halo*'s Cortana is a good example of this. This enables the player's dominance over the real-time game space to remain unchallenged. It is unusual to find games where the player's actions are sidelined, or of lesser importance or perceived value or power—but the very fact that FPS games exist that directly challenge the traditional notion of a powerful central avatar who responds effectively and righteously to the challenging of the correct order of the world requires examination. As a lead into this, consider the central ludic issue at stake: increases in a player's skill at manipulating pattern configurations, or applying affordances, form the core short-scale reward/feedback systems of most digital games. In an FPS game, this short-scale loop is traditionally combat. Combat lets the player evaluate their skills; gibbing and headshots offer instant reward. Getting through a firefight with minimal damage, with an economic use of bullets, or by pulling off a particularly brutal combo, scattering viscera to the corners of the screen—these are rewards, and they hardwire power to the center of traditional FPS gameplay. So what happens to the FPS experience if this capability is destabilized or subverted or removed altogether? Can a game that attacks such a hallowed relationship remain workably engaging?

Consider Frictional Games's *Penumbra* series. With an emphasis on stealth and physics-based puzzles, *Penumbra* offers a degree of largely unsatisfactory combat in *Overture* (2007), which was replaced in *Black Plague* (2008) with simply avoiding or running away from agents. Unlike in *Condemned*, the avoidance of ballistic combat is not replaced in *Black Plague* by moving the gameplay loop to melee. There are no blood spurts and crunching bones, with the result that combat is, simply, deeply unrewarding. *Black Plague* offers no rewards at all, only punishments, for engaging with enemy agents. This radically inverts the normal power relationship: players are confronted, on a short-scale loop, with their own powerlessness. If they are to save this world, they cannot do so by being "good" at the game. More recently, Frictional takes this idea to even greater levels with *Amnesia*, which replaces combat with the considerably less glamorous activity of hiding in cupboards whenever a monster is near. The early stages of *Call of Cthulhu: Dark Corners of the Earth* attempt something similar: even when the player acquires a firearm, combat is messy and unrewarding. Indeed, the game's inability to sustain itself in later sections is largely due to its reduction to a traditional FPS structure that is undermined by a combat system incapable of delivering the rewards normally associated with that type of activity. My own *DOOM 3* mod *Conscientious Objector* (thechineseroom 2008) rewrites the opening levels of the shooter by arming the player with a shotgun that only fires rubber bullets, meaning that the short-scale feedback loop of combat is subverted by having Zombies get back up after being shot down. It was noted that this made it a brutal, nihilistic experience (Burch 2009).

In all three of these games, the avatar is fundamentally challenged as a powerful figure in the world, and the player's actions in this short-scale system are undermined. What results instantly is an increase in tension, and other content, whether it is ludic or diegetic, is required to expand and fill the vacuum. But it is important to note that these games operate by removing the player's ability to obtain rewards from acting skillfully in the space: succeeding in the game is not as simple as mere power playing. For example, *Mirror's Edge* and *Portal* both eschew combat in favor of alternative short-scale loops: reactive free running and physics puzzling, respectively. In both cases, there is a direct parallel to more tactical shooters—and a step back toward the arcades. An approach is planned, and then action is started. Once the action is underway, the focus shifts to reaction speed and skill in responding to circumstance efficiently (and, it should be noted, often aesthetically) in order to configure the best way and receive a rewarding outcome. This is even more the case in melee-based first-person games, such as *Zeno Clash* (ACE 2009) or *Condemned,* where, once again, although guns are replaced by fists and improvised weapons, the basic notion of a skilled manipulation of a presented pattern of stimuli leading to reward is central to the experience. *Penumbra* and the like radically attack this idea, making the application of skill much harder, less rewarding, and more instance-specific—being good at one set of actions in one level does not necessarily translate to being good at another set of actions later on. *Conscientious Objector* is an exception to this, as it embraces the action-reward feedback loop but undermines the reward to force the player to confront an inevitable loss as the game progresses.

There are modern games that don't take quite as radical a stance, fusing diegetic experimentation with traditional gameplay. *Far Cry 2* and *Bioshock* achieve the fusion of diegetic complexity with prototypical genre features. These games are increasingly typical of the genre, rather than obscure or left-field experiments. One has only to scan down the list of recently re-leased AAA titles to witness this significant maturation of the genre. It is important to note that this is a fusion of complexity and difference with the ludic activity prototypical to the genre (both games, after all, are fun-damentally driven by high-octane combat). It is equally important not to underestimate how effectively other titles, such as *Crysis,* create simpler but nonetheless extremely well-crafted action/sci-fi B-movie variations. Having said that, it is now more the case that the supernatural Nazis of the recent *Wolfenstein* remake are *unusual* in their simple diegetics than the *norm.* This is not to say that machine-gunning a room full of glowing skeletal SS officers has lost any of its appeal. Rather, there is evidently now more room in the genre for the same officers to suffer existential crises, for the player to adopt a more complex moral and ethical position relative to them, or even for the world to be turned on its head in a manner that would not shame another media form or audience.

Retro shooters like *Wolfenstein* and *Painkiller* are keeping up a tradition of self-knowing, tongue-in-cheek mindless violence that stretches back to *Serious Sam* (Croteam 2001), *Duke Nukem 3D,* and beyond. But these ludic equivalents of the once ubiquitous Schwarzenegger and Seagal movies are being supplemented by a range of mainstream titles that owe as much to *Heart of Darkness* (Conrad [1902] 2007), *Roadside Picnic* (Strugatsky and Strugatsky 1972), and *Atlas Shrugged* (Rand [1957] 2007) as to anything else. The core qualities of the prototypical shooter are being challenged along the way, with renewed interest in investigating the complexities of ambiguity, power, consequence, isolation, reward, and politics that this genre has a unique capacity to explore. Does all of that mean that *DOOM,* brilliant as it is, is simply a piece of gaming history, or can we find it's dark influence even in the most aberrant, far-flung reaches of the modern FPS? The games there tend to be slower, more about tactics than skill, more com-plex in world and story—even, in many cases, apparently owing as much to *Ultima Underworld* as to *DOOM.* Where have all the demons gone?

CHAPTER 16

SCARYDARKFAST

The Legacy of DOOM

The demons have not gone far, as it turns out. The bottom line is that games are evolving more rapidly than any other medium on the planet right now. However, if FPS games have, in many aspects, gone beyond the template *DOOM* established, it doesn't mean they owe that game any less of a debt. *DOOM*'s contribution to gaming cannot be limited to the idea of a nucleating game, even though the argument that it spawned a genre is very strong. As I hope I've made clear in this book, *DOOM*'s legacy operates along so many fronts simultaneously that its creation of an experiential template for not just first- but third-person shooters is only one of its facets, only one of its achievements.

DOOM brought binary space partitions to games, a seismic step forward in rendering speed, ushering in console and arcade-style play on PCs. It broke new ground with the conceptual compromising of traditional virtual reality to achieve speed and fluidity. It sat at the center of the creation of both the online multiplayer *and* player-generated content worlds. It was perhaps the pinnacle of the shareware/retail distribution model and stands as one of independent game development's towering achievements. It heralded giants of game design and technology into the medium and remains a profound vision of what games do better than anything else: fusing technological advance with creative vision. It is an exceptional case study of fine detail—weapons balancing, level flow, audio design and placement—operating seamlessly with core vision. This vision, this art direction, was darker, faster, more urgent, and more frightening than pretty much anything that had gone before, and yet the game kept that edge of humor that is lacking from the overwhelming majority of modern FPS games. It took play seriously, but it never overstepped its arcade roots.

Then we have the design, on multiple levels. The fusion of science fiction with supernatural horror was nothing new, of course, but it was certainly novel applied in gaming. Adrian Carmack and Kevin Cloud may just be responsible for creating an entire gaming aesthetic, and that's a huge achievement, on a par with the game's technological breakthroughs. Coupled with the inherently immersive qualities of first-person gameplay, *DOOM* pitched players into the dark, where the experience was never diluted by having to engage with complex gameplay or controls. As Romero says, "Sometimes simple is great" (JR).

DOOM is a profoundly lean, economical piece of game design, honed and distilled down to a fine edge. This is fundamentally anchored in the marriage of engine and gameplay design: the design is built to optimize the engine's capabilities, and the engine was built to do just what the design required. It may sound trite or simplistic but *DOOM*'s lesson for any aspiring game developer is the importance of bedrock over blue sky, of doing the basics brilliantly. It boils back down to Kevin Cloud's comment quoted earlier: "Fundamentally, if in a shooter, running and shooting isn't fun, then you're screwed" (KC).

DOOM was hugely ambitious, but what is really telling about its early development is how much was removed from the game to refine the experience. If it didn't work 100 percent, it didn't go in. Despite Romero claiming id "got super lucky" *when* they "super nailed" the balance of the game, and despite knowing just how fast the thing was put together, the id development team demonstrated a singular vision and obsessive drive toward this pure arcade form, reinvented in a 3D PC game that resulted in this beautifully balanced experience. If, as Willits argues, we should be careful not to overassign a grand plan to the development experience, the fact that many of these decisions were made on an instinctive level should be taken as further proof of the talents of those responsible. At the same time, however, *DOOM* didn't come out of nowhere, and both Hall and Carmack point to the flow-through of ideas from *Hovertank 3D* onward, which, in Carmack's words, "allowed us to have already figured out what the important things were" (JC). Hall expands on that.

> [We] tried making every kind of game there was. It allowed us to boil down some great stuff. We made a bunch of games before getting to-

gether, a bunch of small games together, then formed id. That much practice out of the public eye is sort of the way the Beatles did it. Not that we planned that—just worked out that way! (THa)

Certainly, the *DOOM* phenomenon was partially a cultural thing: the Apogee model created a snowballing cult of PC gamers online just ready for a game like *DOOM* to slot into things, and the multiplayer modes of *DOOM* absolutely delivered what they were waiting for. Equally, the fact that the members of the id team were so open in terms of relating to their audience and in allowing the community unprecedented access to their build tools, essentially kick-starting the whole user-generated content scene in games, was fundamental to the creation of a whole subculture around the game. Although somewhat outside the scope of this book, even if you ignore the game, the technology, the art, and the design, *DOOM* is still an important cultural artifact, in terms of its phenomenal visibility and impact. But it's the game's legacy we're after here, and if this cannot be limited to nucleating a genre, then, equally, we need to recognize that it did just that very thing. Both John Carmack and John Romero are clear on this. In Romero's words, "Here it is, the FPS. *DOOM* really created the genre" (JR). Carmack is predictably measured.

It's a stable genre now. Just like forever after we will have driving games and fighting games, there will be first-person shooters forever. Instigating a genre like that is a good thing. I'm proud of that. (JC)

Whichever way you want to look at it, despite Carmack's insistence that if id Software hadn't done it, someone else would, the FPS genre may not have got off the ground at all or may have taken a wildly different direction without *DOOM*. As I've argued in the last chapter, that's not to underplay the role of the first-person RPG or to fail to recognize the evolution since, but there's no avoiding the fact that *DOOM* was the powder keg. If it was a product of many converging historical forces, it still outstrips the argument that it was an inevitable product of the time, by doing so many *new* things so well: mods, shareware, art direction, tech, experimental design. It's also really important to remember that *DOOM* tapped into deep, underlying principles of imagination and play. Kevin Cloud sums this up exceptionally well.

From my perspective, almost every truly popular game derives itself from something kids have been doing or playing forever. So whether you're building something, racing something, blowing something up, these are things that kids do, . . . get a stick, dress up, playing a knight in shining armor. These are all things that we do, and they evolve into these new forms. They find their way into these new forms of entertainment. People want to play the hero. They like the idea of being that guy who is taking on the bad guys—with a kick-ass arsenal—and being able to do it. And to have that kind of feel and connection, that visceral feel, the design is more impacting physical things—sweaty palms, jumping back in your chair—rather than just cognitive stuff. FPS—that's what they do really well. And *DOOM* just hit it. (KC)

Like John Carmack famously said, "You can dress it up in many ways, but the game still comes down to go here, touch this, go there, fight, et cetera" (JC). *DOOM* is a work of profound importance in the history of games not because of one thing it did right but because of many—some groundbreaking, some incremental. At root, this is a game that is based around simple things executed brilliantly, and that's not to infer in any way that simple things are easy to do. This book has, I hope, captured the spirit of the game and made the case (if making it were really necessary) that *DOOM* represents the very best of the core qualities that make games so exciting and important. It's savage, funny, violent, smart, dumb, simple, and complex. It's scarydarkfast. And if you don't believe me, I've got a fistful of vertebrae and a headful of mad, and I'm willing to argue it out on a death-match server of your choice. Because that's just the way we roll here. See you in Hell.

Notes

INTRODUCTION

The subtitle is a tagline for an *Ultimate DOOM* publicity poster seen hanging on the wall of id Software's offices.

1. Strafing, for the uninitiated, is just a fancy term for sidestepping. It is one of the fundamental skills to learn if you want to succeed at high levels of difficulty or in a deathmatch.

2. I should note that this isn't mouselook—the avatar's vision is hardwired to its physical orientation. Mouselook, now a standard feature of FPS games, arrived later courtesy of games like *Marathon* (Bungie 1995), via the strange stepping-stone of key-based "vertical look" features. It's an interesting historical case study: playability potentially decreased during this interim period, as the fast-moving nature of gameplay had to factor in what is quite a complicated additional key-binding set. But that's a subject for another book.

3. http://www.vgchartz.com/game/6232/doom/.

4. This is from http://DOOM.wikia.com/wiki/DOOM.

CHAPTER 1

1. Colley 2004.

2. From a 2001 article, where he also offered five hundred dollars to anyone who could prove him wrong: http://web.archive.org/web/20010410145350/http://www.geocities.com/jim_bowery/spasim.html.

3. Unless otherwise cited, all quotes of John Romero are taken from an interview conducted on June 22, 2010. Throughout, all quotes from that and other interviews are initialized for clarity.

CHAPTER 2

The title is attributed to John Carmack.

1. Given that the focus of this book is on the game itself, Jay Wilbur, as id's business manager at the time, doesn't figure prominently. Let's just confirm his contribution quite simply: no Wilbur, no business, no id, no *DOOM*. Hopefully that clears that up.

2. While writing this book, I attended John Sharp and Richard Lemarchand's 2010 IndieCade panel session, which made a very similar argument for indie development in general.

3. Unless otherwise cited, all quotes of Todd Hollenshead are taken from an interview conducted on March 25, 2011.

4. This is according to Kushner. According to id's website, the company takes "its name from Freud's primal, instinct-driven face of the human psyche," http://www .idsoftware.com/business/history (retrieved on August 6, 2010).

5. In a similar vein to Carmack's comment, it is interesting that developers still feel the need to put something approximating a story into what really just amount to arcade twitch shooters. *Painkiller* and *Unreal Tournament III* (Epic Games 2003) are also good examples. *Wolfenstein 3D* is probably as close to the arcades as it gets in terms of just screaming "Maze! Guns! Nazis!" and leaving the player to it, and much as I love *Bioshock, S.T.A.L.K.E.R.: Shadow of Chernobyl* (GSC Game World 2007), and *Deus Ex*, it's downright refreshing to not have to bother with any kind of story.

6. Unless otherwise cited, all quotes of John Carmack are taken from an interview conducted on March 24, 2011.

CHAPTER 3

1. Available at http://5years.doomworld.com/doomBible/.

2. Unless otherwise cited, all quotes of Tom Hall are taken from an interview conducted on September 3, 2010.

3. According to the Bible, the latter allowed users "to convert captured video images and other NeXT-generated images into a VGA format, move them around, and save them for use on the IBM" (to give you an idea of what that's all about).

4. It's convention that *DOOM*'s levels are referred to by their episode number and then level number. So E1M1 means Episode 1, mission 1. Levels were also named, so while I'll generally use the index code, I will occasionally also use the level name, for readability.

5. In their 2011 *DOOM* postmortem for GDC, available at http://www.gdcvault .com/play/1014627/Classic-Games-Postmortem.

6. This remark is all the more interesting when we consider the preexisting structural constraints for the game given its likely distribution through the Apogee model (see chapter 7 for details).

7. As far as academic discussion goes, my recommendation would be Gordon Calleja's *In-Game* (2011).

8. All quotes of Kevin Cloud are taken from an interview conducted on March 24, 2011.

9. http://toastytech.com/DOOMa/index.html. You can also download the alphas and betas from here.

CHAPTER 4

1. Most famously, the Phobos Base appears to be located in the vicinity of Yangshuo Cavern, China.

2. Actually, *Mirror's Edge* is better thought of as a driving game with combos.

CHAPTER 5

1. The stats that follow are taken from the *DOOM* Wiki (http://DOOM.wikia.com, various contributors and dates) and the *DOOM* Weapon Damage Information page (Bell 1997), http://www.gamers.org/pub/idgames/lmps/tyson/weapons.html (retrieved September 15, 2010).

2. Sandy Petersen has said that Romero was fond of breaking whatever rules about item placement (among other things) were agreed by the design team, so the weapon leaking might reflect that as much as anything else. He says that Romero "constantly broke what few rules we had. For instance, I was told early on that we were saving the chainsaw for the later episodes and that the first episode wouldn't have it. But, of course, John put it in some of his levels (in secret places at least). I'm not dissing him for this—he knew when to break rules, and that was one of his strengths." All quotes of Sandy Petersen are taken from an interview conducted on February 7, 2011.

CHAPTER 6

1. All quotes of Bobby Prince are taken from an interview conducted on February 9, 2011.

2. Arguably, the two are more related than we might immediately suspect. This kind of interconnectivity forms the basis of Douglas Hofstadter's classic 1979 work *Gödel, Escher, Bach,* for example.

3. Colleen Macklin, interview at IndieCade 2010, October 9. The mind boggles over what kind of game DOOM would be if the dominant musical force was Prince rather than thrash.

4. "The Impossible Planet" (directed by James Strong, aired June 3, 2006), in which the Doctor discovers Satan is chained in a pit at the center of a planet orbiting a black hole.

CHAPTER 7

1. http://www.humblebundle.com/.

CHAPTER 8

1. *DOOM* has five difficulty settings: I'm Too Young to Die; Hey, Not Too Rough; Hurt Me Plenty; Ultra-Violence; and Nightmare. The first halves the damage a player takes; the others adjust the numbers and types of monsters. Nightmare disables cheats, increases the speed of monsters, and adds respawning monsters to every level.

2. http://DooMedsda.us/wad947.html.

3. http://speeddemosarchive.com/DOOM.html.

4. http://www.youtube.com/watch?v=KN0K58EfJSg.

5. Originally in the shape of a swastika. This was changed in the 1.666 patch to enable a German release.

6. http://www.computerandvideogames.com/58157/features/games-that-changed-the-world-DOOM/ (retrieved January 26, 2011).

CHAPTER 9

1. All quotes of Sandy Petersen are taken from an interview conducted on February 7, 2011.

2. Every monster has a pain chance percentage when taking damage. If pain kicks in, the monster is paralyzed briefly, unable to fire back at the player. This means that high-rate-of-fire weapons like the chaingun or plasma gun are particularly effective when tackling large tough creatures like the Cacodemon, as they reduce the number of projectiles likely to be flying in the player's direction. For example, the Cacodemon has a high chance (50 percent) of being paralyzed for 6 tics (each tic is worth one thirty-fifth of a second). So if it's taking just under 9 hitscans a second from a chaingun, the chances of compromising its attacks with pain responses are actually quite high. Figuring out how the pain responses work was a skill *DOOM* players could learn in order to give themselves a distinct advantage in combat.

3. I'd love to be able to provide a full and definite list of the order of level creation, but as many parts were recycled during early builds and as no official records were kept, all we have to go on are the memories of the designers.

CHAPTER 10

1. In one of those lovely little moments of media crossover, *Slough* is the name of a famously nondescript English town, immortalized in John Betjeman's 1937 poem so titled: "Come friendly bombs and fall on Slough! / It isn't fit for humans now."

2. Other special weapons that did not make it in are the Dark Claw (described as "silent but deadly," which suggests a stealth weapon and, hence, the need for stealth), the Probieticle (a weapon that yields "minimal damage but gives a read out on the enemy," which suggests a more complex, tactical approach to combat), and the Spray Rifle, which fired multiple shots in a wide arc and may therefore be the true inspiration for the final BFG as found in-game.

3. http://www.gamers.org/docs/FAQ/bfgfaq/.

CHAPTER 11

1. One could probably argue, in counterpoint, that Sabre Interactive's *Timeshift* (2007) is a great example of how a pop star mechanic cannot, ultimately, hide mediocrity in the core gameplay. *Timeshift* allowed players to slow, stop, and rewind time in an FPS setting, but this mechanic was ultimately let down by unimaginative de-

sign and lackluster combat. Even with a very smart mechanic at the center, the game quickly dulled into unrewarding and repetitive set pieces.

CHAPTER 12

The title comes from a line in the *DOOM* comic, perhaps the greatest line in a comic ever, courtesy of Steve "Body Bag" Behling and Michael "Splatter" Stewart.

1. In a 1994 interview with *Video Games* magazine, Carmack described SoftDisk as a "klutz of a company who fumbled the opportunity" presented to them with *Catacomb 3D*. Given that take on things, id's moonlighting is fairly understandable.

2. Unless otherwise cited, all quotes of Tom Willits are taken from an interview conducted on March 24, 2011.

3. There is a limited amount written by academics about modding. Sotamaa 2007 is a good place to start, as is Kücklich 2005. This work all tends to focus on mod culture, rather than mods themselves.

4. Technically, Kanyhalos put a lot of this back in. Blowouts became a feature of the sequel *Clear Sky,* and Burers (and Chimeras) appeared in *Call of Pripyat.* You can get the mod at http://stalker.filefront.com/file/Oblivion_Lost;89584 (retrieved July 28, 2011).

5. http://www.DOOMworld.com/vb/DOOM-general/3365-list-of-unofficial-DOOM-add-on-packs/ (retrieved December 10, 2010).

6. According to Romero and Hall, id was approached by Twentieth Century Fox in March 1993 but turned down the offer of making a game based on *Aliens,* because they wanted to keep creative control.

7. Interview conducted on March 25, 2011.

8. http://www.demruth.com.

9. This is from Doug the Eagle and Kansam's own website: http://www.it-he.org.

CHAPTER 13

1. You can watch the YouTube video of the action as proof: http://www.youtube.com/watch?v=I_PDo3V15lY.

2. Note that this is actually less than *Spasim.*

CHAPTER 14

1. The ban on the original and *DOOM II* in Germany was finally lifted on August 30, 2011, after an appeal from id's new owners, ZeniMax. Source: http://www.usk.de/en/search-for-title/search-for-title/?tx_uskdb_list[action]=search&tx_uskdb_list[controller]=Title&cHash=b702b0e569fc0b029fa8a704e0a58d1b (retrieved September 3, 2011).

2. You can find it at http://www.gamers.org/docs/FAQ/doomfaq/.

3. http://classicdoom.com/doomcomp.txt.

4. Hall recalls, "My *DOOM* Bible detailed a progression from earth to hell to earth-corrupted-by-hell, which is the most disturbing. . . . And that's funny since they did finish that arc in *DOOM II*" (TH). This is discussed in more detail in chapter 4.

5. http://www.vgchartz.com/game/6233/doom-ii/.

6. Id Games Discussion/ *Ultimate DOOM* thread on rome.ro: http://rome.ro/smf/index.php/topic,1525.msg31924/topicseen.html#msg31924 (retrieved July 6, 2002).

7. http://rome.ro/lee_killough/.

8. http://www.idsoftware.com/iphone-games/doom-classic/doomdevelopment.htm.

9. If you are really desperate, you can find all the proper details in the the further reading section at the end of this book and hunt them down yourself.

10. The full text is available here: http://www.doomworld.com/files/doom3faq.shtml.

11. This is according to Steven L. Kent in the id-approved (and co-credited) *The Making of* DOOM 3 (Kent 2004, 180).

12. http://ducttape.glenmurphy.com/.

13. In fact, id remedied the see-or-shoot in 2012's re-release, the *DOOM 3* BFG Edition by adding an armour-mount3ed flashlight. Even knowing that the original mechanic was a PR spin on an engine limitation, it's difficult not to see this as a big cop out for wimps. For me, see-or-shoot may have been an accident, but it's part of what makes *DOOM 3* work, and the game is significantly less frightening when you've got an always-on flashlight.

14. http://www.vgchartz.com/game/7289/doom-3/.

CHAPTER 15

1. I'm not the only one to have suggested using affordances to look at games. Linderoth and Bennerstedt 2007 is worth reading, and it's not a long way from Perron's "gameplay cycle" (2006) or Lindley's "gameplay gestalt" (2002) either.

2. That's not to say it's an easy process. A lot of what follows is based on a very long process of collecting data from a very large number of FPS games over the last six or seven years. Part of that process, along with a big lump of baseline data, an analysis of it, and an argument for why story is best understood as a function of gameplay (based on affordances) can be found in my PhD thesis (Pinchbeck 2009c), available online at http://www.thechineseroom.co.uk/thesis.pdf.

3. We could argue that the ability to jump, for example, is actually a huge change in the available affordances in terms of how it lets a player interact with a world, so it may be a mistake lumping *DOOM* and *Quake* together in this instance.

4. Both *Left 4 Dead* and *Counter-Strike* have the capacity for the player to play alone, essentially as a single player, but *Left 4 Dead's* single-player experience is merely an attempt to recapture the multiplayer experience. *Counter-Strike* is entirely geared toward multiplayer gameplay (*Counter-Strike: Condition Zero* [Sierra Entertainment 2004] does contain a single-player campaign, but it's hardly a significant aspect of the franchise).

5. Or, in the case of *Modern Warfare 2,* multiple roles. It is also worth noting that *Modern Warfare 2,* for all its gung ho, guns-and-ammo gameplay, actually has a plotline centered around an out-of-control hawkish general, a classic "enemy within" story line that is highly critical of "big government."

Glossary

affordance: A feature of an object, the "what it lets you do." For example, a window may be defined by its physical characteristics (height, width, etc.), but it can also be defined by the fact that it "affords" us the ability to see from one room to another while retaining a physical separation. In terms of games, a console's controller affords us the ability to give many differentiated inputs to the system, a monitor affords us a visual representation of the game state, an avatar's controls afford us the ability to influence the game state, and so on.

binary space partition (BSP): A way of describing the associations between objects to be rendered in a game engine, analogous to an index in a book. Rather than render every object and potentially do unnecessary work by rendering objects that are obscured by others, the BSP table can be consulted, redundancy can be avoided, and the rendering process can be speeded up.

boss: A boss is bigger, smarter, and harder to kill than other enemies or monsters. It is normally met at the end of a level and has to be defeated to pursue the journey.

deathmatch: A form of multiplayer gaming where all the players are pitched against each other. The winner is usually either the last man standing, the player with the highest number of kills within a time limit, or the first player to reach a preset number of kills. Team deathmatch is a variation that adds cooperation between players and is the basic model behind the overwhelming majority of multiplayer games and game modes.

diegesis (diegetic/nondiegetic): The world in which a story takes place, made up of everything that the characters who live in that world can experience. For example, the music played by musicians appearing in a film is said to be diegetic and can be heard by the other characters in the film, while the film's soundtrack and credits, which the audience sees and hears but the characters cannot, is said to be nondiegetic.

first-person perspective: A perspective that shows the game world as if seen through the eyes of the player character.

first-person shooter (FPS): A genre of action games defined by the direct mapping of the player's perception onto the avatars. In other words, the avatar is only mini-

175

mally represented, usually by a gun or hands at the bottom of the screen, and the player is invited to look "through" the eyes of the avatar. In recent years, this designation has often been replaced with the more generic "first-person game," to recognize the increase in numbers of games that do not have combat as the central mechanic, such as *Portal, Amnesia,* or *Mirror's Edge.*

frag (fragging): Killing, usually used in the context of killing another player in a deathmatch setting.

frames per second (fps): The number of times everything visible on the screen is redrawn to register changes in the game state (monsters moving, missiles being tracked, etc.). A game's fps rate is often seen as something of a holy grail in action gaming, as it defines how responsive the game is and how smoothly it moves. A low fps rate makes play shuddery and unresponsive and is normally caused by an overloading of the rendering capability of the engine and platform. BSPs work to reduce this slowdown.

gib (gibbing): The bloody lumps scattered around when a monster takes a huge amount of damage in one go and explodes (usually from a rocket launcher or similar weapon). This provides a more rewarding visual kill than normal.

heads-up display (HUD): An overlay on the game's action that gives information to the player about the game state. This is normally nondiegetic, although there has been a trend in recent years to integrate the HUD within the diegetic representation. Normal elements in an FPS HUD include counters for health, ammo, armor, and keycards.

ludic: Of a game. For example, we could speak of a game's ludic elements to refer to those aspects of it that directly pertain to its gamelike nature, such as integer-based health counters or control systems. This is sometimes used to distinguish such elements from diegetic ones in order to irritate game studies researchers.

MIDI: Musical instrument digital interface. Rather than sending audio, a MIDI signal sends information, which can be used to trigger other devices. So a MIDI keyboard could be used to trigger a sampler or a sound card. It is best thought of as a method for creating digital audio.

mod: Modification. A new game created by adapting the code and/or assets of an existing one.

monster closet: A small room that is placed in a map but is inaccessible to the player and normally not signposted with a door. It contains a monster (or several) and is triggered by the player moving around the map—normally opening right behind the player. It is a tried-and-tested method for scaring the living hell out of the player but is sometimes decried as an overused and unsubtle design trick. It still works though.

non-player character (NPC): A game world character that is not controlled by the player.

player character: The main character of the game, whose point of view and body is that of the gamer when he or she plays.

port: A version of a game re-created on a new platform. A ported game normally retains most, if not all, of the original game's features. For example, we would describe *DOOM* on Xbox as a port, as it's essentially the same game. *DOOM 64* for the Nintendo 64, however, is substantially different to the original in many ways, and it may not be appropriate to describe it as such.

role-playing game (RPG): A story-based game where the gamer creates his or her character and chooses the specific role he or she wants to play. The gamer's actions and decisions will change and increase the competence and/or aspect of the character, as well as the course of the story.

shareware: Software that may be freely distributed, normally with a request for donations. Shareware is often part of a larger commercial application, with key features, such as saving files, locked.

speedrun: The practice of trying to complete a game level in the fastest possible time. There are different variations depending on the constraints attached to the run (without taking damage, including killing all monsters, etc.).

texture mapping: Assigning two-dimensional images to the planes of a three-dimensional polygon to create the illusion of detailed environments.

third-person perspective: A perspective that shows the game world as if seen through the eye of a virtual camera, showing the player character in the scene.

References

Atkins, D. 1994. Review of *DOOM*. *Compute!* 163 (April 1994): 82.

Bateman, C., and R. Boon. 2006. *21st Century Game Design*. Boston, MA: Charles River Media.

Bittanti, M. 2006. "From Gunplay to Gunporn: A Technovisual History of the First-Person Shooter." http://www.mattscape.com/images/GunPlayGunPorn.pdf.

Burch, A. 2009. "Indie Nation #64: Conscientious Objector." http://www.destructoid .com/indie-nation-64-conscientious-objector-135226.phtml. Retrieved November 25, 2010.

Calleja, G. 2011. *In-Game*. Cambridge, MA: MIT Press.

Colley, S. 2004. "Stories from the Maze War 30 Year Retrospective: Steve Colley's Story of the Original Maze." http://www.digibarn.com/history/04-VCF7-MazeWar/sto ries/colley.html. Retrieved June 4, 2010.

Conrad, J. (1902) 2007. *Heart of Darkness*. London: Penguin Classics.

Dunnigan, J. F. 2000. *The Complete Wargames Handbook*. 2nd ed. New York: William Morrow.

Foley, J. D., A. van Dam, S. K. Feiner, and J. F. Hughes. 1990. *Computer Graphics: Principles and Practice*. Reading, MA: Addison Wesley.

Ford, N. 2000. "The History of Shareware & PsL." http://www.asp-software.org/users/ history-of-shareware.asp. Retrieved September 16, 2010.

Gibson, J. J. 1979. *The Ecological Approach to Visual Perception*. London: Lawrence Erlbaum Associates.

Kasavin, G. 2004. Review of *DOOM 3* Gamespot, August 5, 2004. http://uk.gamespot .com/pc/action/doom3/review.html. Retrieved December 4, 2010.

Kent, S. L. 2004. *The Making of* DOOM 3. London: McGraw-Hill/Osborne.

Knopf, J. 1995–96. "The Origin of Shareware." http://www.asp-software.org/users/ history-of-shareware.asp. Retrieved September 16, 2010.

Kücklich, J. 2005. "Precarious Playbour: Modders and the Digital Games Industry." *Fibreculture* 5. http://journal.fibreculture.org/issue5/kucklich.html. Retrieved June 22, 2011.

Kushner, D. 2003. *Masters of* DOOM: *How Two Guys Created an Empire and Transformed Pop Culture.* London: Random House.

Linderoth, J., and U. Bennerstedt. 2007. "This Is Not a Door: An Ecological Approach to Computer Games." In *Proceedings of DiGRA 2007: Situated Play,* ed. A. Baba et al., 600–609. Tokyo: University of Tokyo Press.

Lindley, C. 2002. "The Gameplay Gestalt: Narrative and Interactive Storytelling." In In *Computer Games and Digital Cultures: Conference Proceedings,* ed. F. Mäyrä, 203–16. Tampere: Tampere University Press.

Lombardi, C. 1994. "*DOOM II:* The Madness Continues." In *Computer Gaming World* 124 (November 1994): 98–102.

Mäyrä, F. 2008. *An Introduction to Game Studies.* London: Sage.

Naylor, B. 1981. "A Priori Based Techniques for Determining Visibility Priority for 3-D Scenes." PhD diss., University of Texas at Dallas.

Nieborg, D. B. 2004. "America's Army: More than a Game?" In *Bridging the Gap: Transforming Knowledge into Action through Gaming and Simulation,* ed. T. Eberle and W. C. Kriz. Munich: Ludwig Maximilians University. http://www.gamespace .nl/content/ISAGA_Nieborg.PDF. Retrieved June 20, 2011.

Perron, B. 2006. "The Heuristic Circle of Game Play: The Case of Survival Horror." In *Gaming Realities: A Challenge of Digital Culture,* ed. M. Santorineous, 65–66. Athens: Fournos.

Pinchbeck, D. 2007. "Counting Barrels in *Quake 4:* Affordances and Homodiegetic Structures in FPS Worlds." In *Proceedings of DiGRA 2007: Situated Play,* ed. A. Baba et al., 8–14. Tokyo: University of Tokyo Press.

Pinchbeck, D. 2009a. "An Affordance Based Model for Gameplay." In *Proceedings of DiGRA 2009: Breaking New Ground.* London: Brunel University. http://www. digra.org/dl/display_html?chid=http://www.digra.org/dl/db/09287.31155.pdf.

Pinchbeck, D. 2009b. "An Analysis of Persistent Non-Player Characters in the First-Person Gaming Genre, 1998–2007: A Case for the Fusion of Mechanics and Diegetics." *Eludamos: Journal of Computer Game Culture* 3, no. 2: pp 261–79.

Pinchbeck, D. 2009c. "Story as a Function of Gameplay in First-Person Shooters and an analysis of FPS Diegetic Content, 1997–2008." PhD thesis, University of Portsmouth.

Rand, A. (1957) 2007. *Atlas Shrugged.* London: Penguin Classics.

Rehak, B. 2007. "Of Eye Candy and id: The Terrors and Pleasures of *DOOM3.*" In *Videogame, Player, Text,* ed. B. Atkins and T. Krzywinska, 139–53. Manchester: Manchester University Press.

Rollings, A., and E. Adams. 2003. *Andrew Rollings and Ernest Adams on Game Design.* Indianapolis: New Riders.

Salen, K., and E. Zimmerman. 2004. *Rules of Play: Game Design Fundamentals.* Cambridge, MA: MIT Press.

Schumacker, R., B. Brand, M. Gilliland, and W. Sharp. 1969. *Study for Applying Computer-Generated Images to Visual Simulation.* Report. U.S. Air Force Human Resources Laboratory. AFHRL-TR-69-14.

Sotamaa, O. 2007. "On Modder Labour, Commodification of Play, and Mod Competitions." *First Monday* 12, no. 9.

Strugatksy, B., and A. Strugatsky. 1972. *Roadside Picnic*. Trans. A. W. Bouis. Newton Abbot: Readers Union.

Walker, B. 1994. "Hells Bells and Whistles: id Software's *DOOM*." *Computer Gaming World* 116 (March 1994): 38–39.

Whitta, G. 1994. Review of *DOOM II*. *PC Gamer,* November 11, 1994, 134.

Young, J. A. 1994. Review of *DOOM*. *Video Games,* December 1994.

Further Reading

You want more? Good, good—as Betruger might croon, his one good eye glazing over in a kind of hellish rapture. This isn't an exhaustive list (we don't have space for that), but it should get you started. Go look here:

http://DOOM.wikia.com/wiki/DOOM—An invaluable resource for all things *DOOM.*

http://www.doomworld.com/idgames/—How many mods do you need?

http://toastytech.com/DOOMa/index.html—Download the alphas and betas here.

http://DooMedsda.us/wad947.html and http://speeddemosarchive.com/DOOM .html—For speedrun archives.

http://classicdoom.com/doomcomp.txt—Ledmeister's exhaustive port documentation.

http://www.gamers.org/pub/idgames/lmps/tyson/weapons.html—George Bell's breakdown of *DOOM* weapon damage.

http://www.gamers.org/docs/FAQ/bfgfaq/—Tony Fabris's extraordinary testament to the BFG.

http://rome.ro/lee_killough/—Lee Killough's *DOOM* archive, including level creditation and more.

http://www.gamers.org/docs/FAQ/doomfaq/—Hank Leukart's FAQ. Worth it for the poem alone.

http://www.doomworld.com/10years/doomcomic/comic.php—The *DOOM* comic. It's like a comic, only with more *DOOM.* All together now: "Dance! Dance, bonedaddy!" etc.

http://www.gdcvault.com/play/1014627/Classic-Games-Postmortem—Hall and Romero talk shop at the 2011 Game Developers Conference.

www.idsoftware.com—It's their game. You ought to think about playing their other stuff, too.

http://rome.ro—Romero is not just an important designer but a wonderful source of history and preservationist info.

www.tomtomtom.com—HallHallHall. Go visit him.

DOOM NOVELIZATIONS

Hugh, D. A., and B. Linaweaver. 1995. DOOM: *Knee-Deep in the Dead.* New York: Pocket Star Books.

Hugh, D. A., and B. Linaweaver. 1995. DOOM: *Hell on Earth.* New York: Pocket Star Books.

Hugh, D. A., and B. Linaweaver. 1996. DOOM: *Infernal Sky.* New York: Pocket Star Books.

Hugh, D. A., and B. Linaweaver. 1996. DOOM: *Endgame.* New York: Pocket Star Books.

Costello, M. 2008. DOOM3: *Worlds on Fire.* New York: Pocket Star Books.

Costello, M. 2009. DOOM3: *Maelstrom.* New York: Pocket Star Books.

DOOM IN BOOKS

There are chapters on *DOOM* in the following:

Loguidice, B., and M. Barton. 2009. *Vintage Games: An Insider Look at the History of* Grand Theft Auto, Super Mario, *and the Most Influential Games of All Time.* London: Focal Press.

Donovan, T. 2010. *Replay: The History of Video Games.* Lewes: Yellow Ant.

And if you read Italian, here's the only other complete book on the subject:

Bittanti, M., and S. Morris, eds. 2005. *Doom: Giocare in prima persona.* Milan: Costa and Nolan.

Index

Made in the USA
Middletown, DE
11 January 2018